reinventing emma

reinventing emma

The inspirational story of
a young stroke survivor

Emma Gee

OPENBOOK CREATIVE

"It's not what happens to you that matters, it's how you choose to deal with it"

Emma Gee

In loving memory of my grandparents, Joy and Charles Robinson – you provided me with a solid foundation and demonstrated how to live according to your values.

To my parents, Lyn and David Gee for your unwavering love and devotion. By your example, you instilled in me such a positive, compassionate and accepting approach to life. The opportunities you provided enabled me to find meaning in my life and pursue my passions. I will be forever grateful to you and the incredible sacrifices you both have made.

This book is also dedicated to all of the people who encounter seemingly insurmountable challenges in life.

Published in 2016 in Australia by Emma Gee

emmag1@iinet.net.au
www.emma-gee.com

Book Production: OpenBook Creative
Cover Design: Anne-Marie Reeves
Cover Photograph: David Gee

Consulting editor: Annie Hastwell
Copyedited by: Ann Bolch

Australia Cataloguing-in-Publication entry

Author: Gee Emma, author.
Title: Reinventing Emma

ISBN: 9781925144291 (paperback)
9781925144307 (ePub)
9781925144314 (.mobi)

Subjects: Subjects: Gee, Emma E.
Cerebrovascular disease—Patients—Australia—Biography.
Occupational therapists—Australia—Biography.
Motivational speakers—Australia—Biography.

Dewey Number: 362.196810092

In order to maintain their anonymity some names of individuals and places have been changed.

CONTENTS

Foreword

What a marvellous thing Emma Gee has done for us in writing her searingly honest account of her extraordinary journey across a decade as she has struggled with courage, hope and determination to recover from a haemorrhagic stroke, to reinvent herself, to keep going day after day through the toughest gullies.

Yes, her story has moments of wry humour, deeply affecting insights, glimpses of joy but again and again, Kipling's words about *"forcing heart and nerve and sinew"* come to mind.

Emma's compelling memoir opens with an almost lyrical account of a charmed childhood, halcyon days at university, overseas travel, confidence growing on the threshold of personal and professional achievements, adventures in spades.

Completely and utterly out of the blue it all began to change. Her very life was threatened. Every aspect thrown into chaos as frightening, confusing, horrific anxiety struck her down. Her body began to deteriorate. The search for a diagnosis and treatment led to brain surgery. Emma suffered a devastating stroke. Her own remembrances and her mother's diary notes of these harrowing experiences are confronting. They bring awareness and understandings that are powerful and instructive, so many painful truths.

We travel beside Emma on her gruelling recovery road. Oh, the tension in her storytelling. Every day was a struggle, *"my wings had been clipped. I may no longer fly"*. Every day terror surrounded and engulfed her.

As an occupational therapist, Emma has insightful and constructive observations to make about the rehabilitation rollercoaster.

This book is confronting, illuminating in its candour and uplifting in its illustration of the inner strength of an exceptional young woman. Love shines through the pages; love and family, her identical twin sister, siblings, partners, little children, enduring friendships. Those through thick and thin devoted parents who gave unstintingly to Emma's future, encouraging her independence.

The wise mother treading on eggshells worrying about being pitying or patronising, who was both in the best way. The father who sat in the wheelchair to make it look normal. How inspiring are these anecdotes of the day to day loving, caring, sharing, grief, loss and joy!

Reinventing Emma must be read by all health professionals and by all of us who want to strengthen our knowledge of our shared humanity.

I am inspired by Emma's forthright advocacy, her description of her gutful of society's misconceptions about disability. I am inspired too by the recovery that came with work and purpose, her public speaking, her mentoring, support and encouragement for stroke survivors.

We must learn from this remarkable book how to offer help, especially to people with disabilities, to be aware of the emotional and financial toll disability imposes and to hold fast to the principles of the human rights doctrine about the dignity and worth of every human being.

Emma, we are indebted to you.

The Honourable Quentin Bryce AD CVO

An inspiring and insightful read. An amazing true story of courage, compassion, and commitment in the face of devastating loss. Emma Gee's story will move you deeply and her resilience will astound you.

Dr Russ Harris, M.B.B.S.
Author of The Happiness Trap

This book is a significant contribution to the 'therapist as patient' literature. At once ferociously intelligent and deeply felt, it is required reading for every health professional, every health consumer.

Nick Rushworth,
Executive Officer
Brain Injury Australia

Reinventing Emma is a moving tribute to the courage of one inspirational young lady who, although representative of many thousands of young people who suffer a stroke, is exceptional because she ***chose*** *to find meaning and purpose from her condition. Her account of the sudden change of life as it once was, along with the partial loss of the very essence of herself, I found compelling. It was evident Emma found herself with two choices – she could spend* *her life mourning the fact that her dreams were now shattered, or do whatever she could to change what could be changed, without forsaking the insight to accept what couldn't. So Emma learnt to push the boundaries of her impairments, and in so doing, she teaches those around her to do the same. Despite living in a society which values status and ability, the way in which Emma reinvents her life, teaches us that individuals should be accepted for who they are and whatever contribution they can make to society. This resilient young lady has reaffirmed my own belief that human development cannot be accurately determined by science, nor can potential be predicted, or spirit measured.*

Cheryl Koenig OAM.
Author & Motivational Speaker

Like Emma, I am an occupational therapist, and I have worked with many stroke survivors. Reinventing Emma taught me many additional things about stroke, including strategies that other stroke survivors [and therapists] can use to improve their quality of life. Emma's book is beautifully written and a pleasure to read with great real-life stories interwoven throughout and will leave you wanting more

Dr Annie McCluskey,
Senior Lecturer in Occupational Therapy,
The University of Sydney

Introduction

I've been on a challenging yet amazing journey over the past ten years. My life has been turned upside down in ways I could never have imagined. In 2005, at the age of 24, I survived a haemorrhagic stroke and went from being a young, sport-loving, professional woman and full-time therapist, to being a helpless, dependent nonentity. Overnight I became a powerless patient, like the ones I had been caring for. The roller-coaster ride that began with a sore knee has led me on a totally unexpected and unimaginably difficult journey. And yet everything, both good and bad, has shown me, surprisingly, what is possible when you accept life's challenges.

The sudden transition from therapist to patient has given me a completely different perspective. When I first reached the point in rehabilitation where I could read and write again, I had a passion to share my insights about life as a patient. I decided that this book would be for other health professionals. With that in mind I started a Masters degree but quickly realised another qualification was not going to help me to impact people as directly as I wanted to. I felt as though I needed to make a difference right now.

I've walked in the shoes of a patient and I want to tell that story. I've realised how much health professionals really don't know about what it's like to be a patient, and how even the little things they do without noticing can affect someone else's path to recovery. I now know so much more about improving the quality of life for patients and their supporters. And the bigger lesson I've learnt, and want to share with everyone, is the importance of resilience when life doesn't go to plan.

It's taken me quite a few years to write this book. Always a keen diarist, I faithfully recorded every amazing and terrible thing happening to my body, from the first mysterious symptoms through to waking up after being in a coma. My writings range from serious attempts at storytelling to scraps, strings of words that were all I could manage at times to describe the nightmare world I had found myself in.

I've heard plenty of inspirational stories, read books and seen movies about people who have survived in the face of great personal odds. Those stories helped me but they also intimidated me a little when it came to writing about my own experience. I don't feel as though I've accomplished an amazing feat and, even though I work as an inspirational speaker, I find the title doesn't sit comfortably. My journey seems more mundane. I've survived and I go on surviving day to day. That is what I want to share. This book is not all about success, but an authentic account of overcoming the difficulties I've encountered and still do encounter every day in my stroke recovery.

This is only *my* experience. Despite undergoing a life-changing event at a young age and learning to live with disability, I could never presume to fully understand how a brain injury may have affected others. A stroke, whenever it happens, is a terrible and life-changing experience. Everybody's story is different and, although we share many struggles with tiredness, and lack of understanding, support and motivation, disability comes in many forms. It can happen at varying life stages and impacts us and those we love in many different ways. I hope my story can help not just those who have gone through their own personal nightmare, but also give some insight and extra understanding to those who love and care for them.

Lying in intensive care I never imagined I would have balance in my life again. In fact, I am dumbfounded that I have been able to reinvent myself and pursue what I love. I have developed amazing relationships, returned to meaningful work, begun my own business and written a book, all while continuing to juggle my seemingly never-ending rehab. But I have learnt that it's not what happens to you that matters, it's how you choose to deal with it.

Chapter 1
Beginnings

"Open your eyes Em!" a voice instructs.

I'm too tired to know what they're asking me to do. I am lying on my right side. All I can taste is blood. All I can feel is cold. All I can hear is my twin sister's nervous chatter and my older sister quietly sobbing. I'd prefer to sleep.

I do.

Again a voice pleads, "Darling, please open your eyes." Now someone's holding my hand, their thumb delicately moving from side to side. It's a familiar voice and a familiar touch. I tell myself to open my eyes. I try but it doesn't work. I'll speak to them later. Right now I need to sleep.

"You're OK, the operation went well," someone is saying, too loudly. I fight my way out of strange nightmarish dreams. I'm cold, tired and I don't like this place so I instruct my body to curl up in a ball and drift back to sleep. But my body won't budge. Perplexed, I try to concentrate harder on moving any body part, *even wriggling my little finger would be* OK. But again my entire body stubbornly remains still and limp. I'm trapped in a bubble inflated by sickly smells of blood and disinfectant. I try to cry out for help but no words come. Nothing works. My body is broken. I can't move or speak. This wasn't what I planned when I made the decision to have this operation.

~

For the 24 years leading up to this, life had been sweet. I entered the world on the 28th of July 1980, seven minutes before my twin sister Bec. I had those minutes alone with my doting parents until the doctor declared, "Bloody hell, there's another one in there!"

Mum gasped, "Another what?"

My shocked Dad murmured, incredulous, "Lyn, we're having twins!"

Unnamed, we were known as 'Twin 1' and 'Twin 2' for three days, and were left in hospital while Mum and Dad bought another one of everything and prepared my two older siblings for the arrival of their twin baby sisters.

Growing up as an identical twin had its good and bad points. I always had someone to play with. From Grade One we were deliberately separated to help us form our own identities. We both had bobbed blonde hair, identical gappy teeth and answered to each other's names. Even our older sister and brother often failed to see us as two separate little individuals. In fact, Mum tells the story about my three-year-old brother Pete lying on the carpet and playing roughly with us when we were just four months old. Mum cautioned him. "Darling, please don't be so rough with the girls, they're only little." Despite her warning he continued to tumble, poke and prod.

"Peter, what did Mum say?" she pleaded, walking over to scoop us up, balancing our fragile bodies on her hips.

Pete grinned and reassured her. "Don't worry Mum, if one cracks open we've always got the other one!"

Little did anyone realise that 24 years later one would 'crack open' and what challenges that would present.

We looked the same, but we could act differently. Bec was strong, stubborn and unstoppable whereas I was the sensitive one. I longed for her strength of character. Bec was always more daring than me in tackling the unknown. She'd jump off diving boards and climb high trees while I hung back.

"Face your fears," she would say to me. One day I would become master of this, but what my sister didn't say was that facing your fears doesn't necessarily make them go away.

One way of overcoming fear is to remember the nice things. My childhood was a huge portion of my disability-free life and so it's a favourite thing for me to remember. A time when I ran from place to place and was just another 'normal' kid. A time when I went around and around the skating rink for fun, when a grazed knee was healed immediately with a kiss better or a Band-Aid.

I remember our neighbourhood as an exciting little world of its own – a kingdom where we kids reigned free and independent. My very favourite people in the street were the Mullins family. They weren't quite next door. There was a house between us but we ignored that and spent most of our time dreaming up ways to connect our houses – flying foxes and underground tunnels. I spent a lot of my childhood playing with the Mullins girls. We had sleepovers, built cubby houses, spent hours playing board games and went on bike rides.

But the biggest influence in my life was my family. There were six of us, my parents and four kids – my older sister Kate, my brother Pete, my twin sister Bec and me. Although we had normal sibling quarrels, we grew up in a loving and nurturing place and came to love and respect each person's individuality. My parents were great role models, their contrary personalities along with their aligned life values balanced perfectly. Mum's a sensitive down-to-earth person, always there for you and very open. Dad is very private, pragmatic and able to distance himself from a situation. At the same time he is very loyal. Their Christian faith was always at the centre of their lives and mirrored in all that they did. They provided us with a secure, accepting environment, at the same time challenging us with new opportunities and adventures. Our parents captured the potential in all four of us and we felt valued and believed in. They ensured we were grounded, exposing us to those less fortunate and in their regular acts of generosity and community involvement they instilled in us a strong sense of personal values. These were never forced upon us. Rather they seemed to subconsciously plant seeds in us, weaving them through the way they went about their lives. As Bec and I were identical twins, they always tried to make each of us feel unique and seemed to effortlessly distribute their overflowing love to all of us kids evenly.

The importance of family was paramount in my mum's childhood, so we spent many holidays with our extended family on my grandparents' farm, 'Springview', in Young, New South Wales. Here there were 1000 acres to explore and have adventures with my cousins.

My grandpa would welcome us with a tight squeeze, clenching his false teeth in preparation and effortlessly lifting our four dangling bodies in unison. Then my aproned grandma would appear and our bellies would soon be full, after consuming her amazing spread of home-cooked food.

On the farm we were invincible and free. I longed to be tough like my country cousins. Each stay I would try my best to push aside any urges of complaining about teeny scratches or fearing getting dirty. We milked cows, fed the foul-smelling pigs, made cubbies in the pine trees and lit bonfires. As city kids we loved doing non-city things like riding motorbikes and running barefoot on dirt tracks. While recalling these times reminds me of all of the things I am no longer able to do, at the same time each memory is precious and makes me appreciate the wonderfully wild and active childhood I was lucky enough to have. In some way each farm trip reset my perspective on life and left me feeling rejuvenated and revived.

Holidays over, I was excited to resume my busy city lifestyle where I took up as many activities as I could manage. From early primary school I learnt classical ballet and loved the discipline, creativity and grace involved in performance. I also fell in love with long-distance running and netball. Throughout high school I became involved in everything. Whether it was drama, dance, music or sport, I tried it. In most school drama productions I was guaranteed a role as a twin. Bec and I played Tweedledee and Tweedledum. In another play we were cast as twin grandmas, delivering our lines in unison. If the script didn't have twin characters, they were added.

In reality, though, by high school Bec and I were starting to form more separate identities, and I was getting a feeling for who I really was. I enjoyed being with people and caring for them. As a lot of my family were in the health professions, and two of my aunties and my older sister were occupational therapists, I started to think about a career in the health sciences.

During those last years at school there were shadows on the horizon. In 1997 my mum was diagnosed with Type 1 Diabetes and later with a cavernous hemangioma (a type of brain tumour that had destroyed her optic nerve, causing her to lose the sight in her right eye). Then my twin sister was hospitalised with a stomach condition and had to have sudden life-threatening surgery. It was my first realisation that life didn't always go according to plan. They both recovered and even though Mum had vision loss and Bec couldn't sit her exams that year, it didn't really affect *my* life hugely. I was House Captain, and finished Year 12 with a score of 93.5. I felt invincible. Nothing was going to get in my way. Career, marriage, children, it all lay ahead. So I thought…

Chapter 2
A Taste of the Future

In 2003, three years into my occupational therapy degree, I decided to take myself off to Tanzania for a few months. Looking back, I can't believe I did this. I'd led a sheltered life and hadn't even done the Europe trip like most of my friends. Mum was very hesitant to let me go and insisted I wear a wedding ring to ward off any admirers. It didn't work. I had 18 marriage proposals in three months! I volunteered as an assistant at the Tuppendane Centre in Maji Ya Chai village, Arusha, where my job was to help care for and educate 70 street children.

Tanzania certainly provided the challenge I was looking for. There was no electricity or water, and my accommodation was a rat-infested concrete blockhouse. The guard of the centre would lock me in at night to keep me safe, but inside was worse than out. I was trapped inside with the furry creatures, and plugging the gaps in the walls with my camping socks didn't deter them. All night rats would squeal and run around the room and clamber up and down my mosquito net as I pelted them with boxes of medication, the only weapons I had. It was a hideously claustrophobic experience that I was to relive in a surreal way years later when I woke up in hospital trapped inside my own body.

Being the only *mzungu* (white person) in the small village, I stood out, something I'm used to now but wasn't then. On my daily walks I was joined by a stream of African children, my blonde hair was patted for good luck and everyone would say, "Good morning to you!" It was the only English phrase they knew and they used it whether it was morning, afternoon or night.

Living in a third world culture was a huge eye-opener. 'Sick days' didn't exist, even though many villagers were constantly suffering from malaria. Complaining, I soon realised, was just not part of their culture. One day I had lunch at a villager's house and was saddened to see his two-year-old son with a severe eye infection. He was too young to complain but even if he was able to I'm sure he would not have mentioned his discomfort. His family couldn't afford medication, and the only way I could help was to buy him eye drops. Now, when I constantly suffer eye infections, I can't imagine letting them go untreated.

Seeing the lives of the children in Africa was like being on another planet. I couldn't believe how sheltered my life had been. Typically I'd pass children on my walk through the village carrying buckets of water on their heads. Four-year-olds would be put in charge of ten cattle and a donkey, with only a stick to control them. Children seemed almost expendable; mothers would plead with me to exchange their newborns for a few dollars so they could buy a bag of rice.

A disabled child was a source of shame. Once I saw an African lady carrying 'dizzies' (bananas) on her head, and carrying a newborn baby on her back covered by a sarong. It was hot and I thought she was protecting him from the heat. Then a local villager approached her and they exchanged words about the new baby. The mother lifted the shield, I assumed to show off her new baby, but both mother and onlooker pointed and laughed at the baby, who had Down Syndrome. He was clearly regarded as a reject.

Another cultural learning curve was when I witnessed one of the 70 orphans in my care, an eight-year-old girl, being sexually abused by a nine-year-old boy. When I told the visiting social worker about it, assuming he'd be shocked and take some kind of action, he just said, "Emma, they are street children, and Amelia is retarded!"

I was outraged at his words. "Well surely that is even more reason to act now!" He didn't seem fazed by my anger and went on crunching on his maize. I couldn't believe he could swallow it.

At the Tuppendane Centre I was quickly thrown in the deep end. A few days after I arrived the head of the centre disappeared with the large sum of money I'd paid to the volunteer organisation. Then the sole nurse left to give birth, leaving me in charge of the health and education of all of the children. Overnight I became nurse, teacher and mother to a wild bunch of non-English-speaking orphans, ranging from toddlers to young adults. With the extra challenge of no water or electricity, my twin sister's motto of 'face your fears' was truly put to the test.

As bad as things were, I was surrounded by uncomplaining Africans, so I really had to rise to the occasion. Before I could get anything done I needed to be able to communicate with the children, so I set about learning some basic Swahili. They had no shoes, so I bought a hundred pairs of *malopas*, the African version of thongs. I also purchased rat-proof barrels in which to keep food, and contacted a toothbrush company in England and asked them to sponsor the centre by sending toothbrushes. Most of the kids had fungal infections on their scalps, so I also launched a haircutting and treatment program.

Living within a very vulnerable community was a huge personal challenge. My experience there unmasked qualities that I didn't know I had. Away from my 'twinness', my dormant stronger attributes, qualities that I had thought only Bec had, revealed themselves. Travelling alone, I was forced to be more direct, strong-minded and assertive. I also saw firsthand the importance of many human skills like communication that I'd taken for granted. When living in Africa I had to rely heavily on facial expressions and body language to work out what was going on around me. In a strange way it was a foretaste of what was to come. Not being able to speak the language made me feel isolated and helpless, like I would later feel when I lost the power of speech.

In Africa I really saw and understood what discrimination means, something I now experience daily because of my disability. The frustratingly slow-paced culture taught me patience, which I've certainly needed through my long months and years of rehabilitation. It was also a real-life lesson in taking the time to understand where the other person was coming from, rather than just acting like the 'expert'. Later, when I became a patient myself, I learnt to value therapists and others who used this empathetic approach.

I only spent three months in Africa but they were intense. What had been seemingly important in the western world became irrelevant. I learnt that when faced with any obstacle and out of your comfort zone, you can still have control over how you choose to deal with things. Their 'live one minute at a time' approach made me see how much I had been focused on acquiring certain possessions, achievements and status before I could be content. The African people had little but it didn't seem to affect their happiness in the present moment.

Chapter 3
Signs of Something Wrong

After those extraordinary three months in Africa I came back keener than ever to finish university and start a career where I could help people and make a difference. I graduated from La Trobe University with a Bachelor of Occupational Therapy (OT). As an OT my role was to get people who had an injury back to engaging in everyday activities. My first job was as a locum at Caulfield General Medical Centre (CGMC), the same place I was to end up as a patient a few years later.

Right from the start I loved my job. Through university I'd worked in a pharmacy and counted the hours and the dollars. As an OT, I was doing something I was passionate about, so being paid seemed like a bonus.

After Caulfield I began working at the Royal Melbourne Hospital where as a new graduate I was rotated through different areas. I worked in rheumatology, back care, pain management, hand therapy and neurology. In back care the caseload was fairly routine work, mainly WorkCover patients. But in neurology the work was much more varied and interesting. I worked with people in their own homes, for example, helping someone with multiple sclerosis relearn how to shower or a hairdresser who had had a stroke relearn how to cut hair. The gains were obvious and rewarding and I enjoyed the holistic nature of the work, being with people in their own environments. I quickly grew to love this area of OT.

By February 2005, though, I was ready for a holiday. I hadn't had one since Africa 18 months earlier, and I felt I needed reviving before giving the new job my best shot. I'd just broken up with my long-term boyfriend and was ready for some quality girl time. With three of my closest friends, Al, Fi and Kiri, I set off to spend two weeks in Sabah, Borneo. It was an active holiday; we climbed mountains, snorkelled off the islands, saw the orang-utans and explored the local markets, enjoying the Malay culture and amazing food.

It was in Malaysia that I began to notice some strange changes in my body. Because we were in the tropics we had to take anti-malarials and I had chosen doxycycline, which has a side effect of light sensitivity and nausea. As well as those symptoms I began to experience back pain and found I was a bit clumsy, but I put it down to the the drug and perhaps just being too relaxed on holiday.

The big thing we all wanted to do on this trip was to climb Mt Kinabalu. It was over 4000 metres high but in the Lonely Planet guide they said the climb was easy and that "Grandmas could do it," so I wasn't worried. I was fit and I had packed knee tape as a precaution because my knees had suffered in the past as a result of netball. We ascended the mountain in silence, like a human snake. I was ahead the whole way, followed by my friends and rounding us up was our porter Ami. All you could hear were our increasing gasps for air. Step by step. It seemed endless. We were told that as the altitude increased, the foliage would change, but I didn't expect bodily changes as well.

The plan was to reach the top of the mountain for sunrise. It was pitch dark. We'd walk ten metres and need to stop to catch our breath. *Grandmas couldn't do this!* I was struggling and we weren't anywhere near the top. I had an excruciating, piercing headache and my left side was painfully freezing. I didn't say anything, partly because I felt paralysed with the pain, but also because I assumed everyone else was feeling the same.

The exhilaration of reaching the top and looking down at the clouds justified the tiredness and pain. Sharing that moment with friends had made the struggle worthwhile. Then of course the exhilaration turned to dread. The saying, "What comes up, must come down," was true. The human snake reversed, and we set about crab-stepping down the mountain. The novice climbers we passed asked, "How was it?" and we replied, "Fine." On the way up we'd asked the same question and got the same white lie reply. There was no point in telling them how hard it was. They had to experience it to truly understand.

After the big climb we had three days of sleeping, snorkelling, diving and eating to get over the ordeal, but my body didn't feel right. I was ultra-sensitive to light, my skin blistering easily, so I decided to go off the doxycycline early. The risk of malaria seemed preferable to these horrible side effects. I was also clumsier than usual but I put that down to being an after effect of the climb. The plane trip home was agony. My neck and back were excruciatingly painful. Unable to sit, I lay on the airport floor and spent the entire flight walking up and down the aisles, while the other girls slept.

The day after my return I started work. In spite of the strange symptoms I'd returned with, I was otherwise brown, rested, refuelled and ready to put lots of energy into my role as a neurological therapist. I didn't realise that it was my own brain that was about to become the centre of attention.

Chapter 4
The Mystery Deepens

After that holiday I felt my real self, independent at last. After a series of back-to-back relationships I was determined that 'boy' issues would no longer dominate my life. I was moving forward.

I began going out more and being more spontaneous. Sport had always been a huge part of my life. Now I'd discovered the thrill of running and was doing regular 15 kilometre runs. I'd recently done a half marathon and was training for the next one. I was playing netball twice a week and enjoying living in a share house and spending lots of time with friends. I loved my present single status.

Work was also a joy, and I was getting more passionate about neurology. One of my patients was a 36-year-old woman who had had a stroke while giving birth. She was battling many physical and cognitive difficulties, but she was soon feeding, holding, dressing and bathing the baby. It was inspiring to see her progress and it definitely confirmed my love for rehab. She was soon home again with her little family, in her own place, where she clearly wanted to be. Seeing her life suddenly turned upside down at such a young age should've shown me that things don't always go the way you plan. But I was too absorbed in my own happily organised world to notice.

Life was good but I was getting increasingly worried about my body. It seemed to be 'out of sync'. I felt as though mentally I had to push my limbs to keep going, and concentrate harder to make my body parts move. When I ran, now I had to focus on each step to make sure it happened. It was no longer automatic. Before this, I had sailed along and let my mind wander on important topics like clothes shopping or where to go for dinner. Movement no longer seemed to come naturally; rather it felt robotic and forced. I was walking weirdly and becoming clumsier, often misjudging distances between objects and running into things, particularly on my right side. My housemate even said one day, "You Ok Em? You're not walking right." I brushed that comment aside and said I was just tired. But his words added to my growing fear that something was really wrong.

My eyes became super-sensitive to light. I couldn't go outdoors without sunglasses and even started wearing them inside when I was alone. The back pain and headaches were the worst. Although I was already very fit, I joined a gym, thinking that a weights regime might help my core stability and strengthen my back. By then painkillers had become part of my daily routine, the strongest 'over the counter' ones I could buy. I was measuring my day in six-hour segments, waiting until I could take the next dose, even though they weren't even touching the pain. I was grumpy and irritable and it began to affect those around me. As well as the pain there was the lack of sleep and, combined with the clumsiness, I was finding it increasingly difficult to function.

After another night of pain and poor sleep I woke on Monday 28th of March 2005 with a weird feeling in my leg. Ignoring it, I got up and picked up a heavy basket of washing to hang out before I went off to start my day's long 'to do' list, which included a 15-kilometre run. As I went down three steps of the internal staircase I heard a distinct 'pop' behind my left knee. It was quite painful. I remember saying to my housemate, "My body's falling apart!"

But I wasn't about to let a sore knee get in the way of my day. I had a string of social occasions before my run and a netball game that night. Off I went to have breakfast and shop with my sister, followed by coffee with friends. By mid-morning I had a little limp. It didn't deter me, but by lunchtime it was becoming worse. As the day went on my jeans were becoming progressively tighter as my knee swelled. Bec thought we should check with Dad, as he's a doctor, so we drove over to my parents' house. Dad suspected a Deep Vein Thrombosis (DVT) and said it should be checked out. My parents had guests over for dinner so Bec offered to drive me to hospital. I still wasn't taking the situation seriously, annoyed that my knee was upsetting the day's plans. On the way to the Emergency Department Bec and I joked about my funeral and who would give my eulogy. Neither of us had any idea how close such things were to coming true.

In Emergency I was asked to fill out a pile of forms. Thankfully, with a straightforward medical history it was quick. I slid the completed documents onto the blue counter and a nurse wheeled a wheelchair into the waiting area.

"A wheelchair," I said, laughing. "I don't need that, I've just got a little limp."

"Sorry Love, it's our policy." She patted the blue vinyl backrest.

"Shouldn't be too long," I said to Bec reluctantly, as I lowered myself gingerly into the chair, swivelling the footplates into the right position.

"Actually, Bec … Maybe get someone to fill in for me tonight at netball? Doubt I'll get there," I called out behind me as the nurse whisked me away to be examined.

When they decided to keep me in overnight for observation, I began to freak out a bit. *I'd have to make up the run I was missing and would definitely need someone to fill in for me at the netball game.* Looking back, I can't believe all the little things that worried me at that moment. As it turned out, I would never run again, never play netball again and indeed never return to my old life.

Later that evening my knee injury was diagnosed through ultrasound as a Baker's cyst rupture, a reasonably common running injury. This explained the pop, the pain and the swelling. My poor mobility seemed secondary to the swelling so it all made sense. But the hospital staff were puzzled that despite my swelling going down, my ability to move had become worse. When they gave me Clexane, a blood thinner to reduce the swelling, it prompted a sudden onset of nausea and left-sided weakness. Soon I was having difficulty walking at all. Concerned at my sudden decline, the staff moved me from Emergency to a room with three elderly ladies. I tried to walk to the bathroom but took one step and fell. Reluctantly, I borrowed a frame from one of the ladies and stumbled to the bathroom. To counter the terror I felt I convinced myself it was merely the swelling that complicated my ability to move and balance.

By this time Mum and Dad had arrived. I was given my second shot of stinging Clexane as my left leg was still quite swollen and I couldn't walk. About 15 minutes later I felt a weird and frightening sensation. I groaned to Mum, "Mum something's wrong, I feel like I'm falling!" I then went sheet white and started throwing up. Indeed, something wasn't right. The nurse was called and I was sent for an MRI scan, with a bucket in hand as I couldn't stop throwing up.

I returned to my room where my mum, dad, sister, a few close friends and my OT manager were waiting. I greeted them not with a "Hi" or a hug but a big black vomit. Not only had my manager never seen me in PJs and without make-up, she'd definitely not seen the 'throwing-up' side of me, but at that moment I really didn't care. Soon I was transferred by ambulance to the Alfred Hospital for further investigation.

I had never been really sick before. I had extras with Medibank Private to cover my few physio and optometry bills, but had decided that I didn't need hospital cover. My rationale was that I'd much prefer to spend that money on a new pair of heels. The price that I would eventually pay for that flippant decision was huge, both financially and emotionally. The cost of that ambulance ride was only the beginning of the medical costs I was about to endure.

Chapter 5
The Alfred – Digging for Reason

At the Alfred Hospital the first nurse took my blood and immediately said in a monotonous, tired, careless tone, "Think you've got diabetes." That was the first of many incorrect diagnoses stamped on my medical file.

That night I wasn't allowed to use the toilet until I'd been assessed, so I held on. At 12.20pm I was getting desperate so I rang the buzzer by the bed.

"You can't leave your bed until you've been examined, so use this pan," the nurse said, wedging a cold, hard metal bedpan underneath me.

"I'll leave you alone to do your business, Love." She drew the thin blue curtain around me. Alone, I tried to balance on top of the harsh bit of equipment. *Even squatting over drop holes in Africa was better than this!* When I finished, I buzzed the call button but no one came. Impatient, I buzzed again, the metal was pinching my skin. I tried to shift my weight without spilling the pan's contents. *The busting feeling was better than this pain.* I sat there in coldness and discomfort for what seemed like hours. Eventually, I heard footsteps enter the room. A young male registrar pulled across the sheer curtain, finding me perched inelegantly on the bedpan. It was my first experience of the indignity of being a patient.

At the Alfred stranger and stranger things began happening to my body. My left toes would claw in, and the sensation on my left side differed from my right side. Constant fuzzy pins and needles radiated down my left leg, which had become heavy and lifeless. None of the experts could work out what was wrong. There was talk of multiple sclerosis, muscular dystrophy and even Guillain-Barre syndrome. I'd had patients with all of these conditions and I was becoming terrified!

As the doctors continued to guess my condition, I struggled to emotionally detach. I focused on each minute and tried hard not to be bogged down with anxiety about my future. I reminded myself, *This is just a brief taste of what many of my patients have to endure for a lifetime*. I focused on what I could learn from the experience.

No longer able to walk, I soon mastered the use of a pick-up stick. I was even able to grab my mobile phone on the other side of the bed with it. But as much as these aids I'd once prescribed for my own patients helped, the many frustrations I encountered made me realise why patients are called 'patients'. Meal trays out of reach and unanswered responses to my many buzzes were just a few things that made me feel increasingly helpless.

In the absence of any diagnosis I was put in the cystic fibrosis ward where there was a free bed. My neighbour, Nora, was full of complaints. At nights, when she did sleep, she breathed so loudly it almost drowned out the constant sputum-coughing soundtrack of that ward. But usually she stayed awake complaining about everything, mainly the position of her pillows. Nora was particularly horrified about the food. It was so hard to keep a straight face when she'd describe her 'meat' meal to her daughter on the phone. "That beef may as well still be running around in the paddock."

One of my first 5pm meals was a boiled chicken; no veggies, just a chicken boiled in its own juices. I could hardly look at it, let alone eat it. If they hadn't beheaded and plucked it free of feathers, I swear you'd think it was still alive. The man next door in Room 23 was clearly not impressed with his meal either, throwing his chicken at a nurse. All you could hear was a crash, a yell and the nurse saying in a resigned voice, "He didn't like the chicken."

I regularly wheeled my way down to the cafeteria for meals or to meet friends there for coffee to escape the endless coughing and try to feel slightly more normal. One day a friend, instead of waiting on me like everyone else, said, "You get the sugar and I'll get the coffee." Wheeling myself across to get that sugar gave me the sugar high I needed. It really hit me that I needed to keep doing all that I could. It taught me the importance of another person's role in helping recovery, the importance of 'doing with' rather 'doing for'.

One of the nicer surprises at that time was the flood of visitors and gifts to my bedside each day. They'd bring flowers, takeaway food and their upbeat attitudes helped me pass the time and remain positive. I confess to being quite humbled by their presence.

"Hey Em." Nina entered the room, giving me a hug and a big sloppy kiss. Nina was my best friend from high school.

"Sorry I'm late, traffic's a nightmare." She perched on the end of my bed, lifted my untouched meal tray, scrunched her nose and said, "Do you have any of that jelly left, I'm starving."

"I saved a green and red jelly for you, it's in the fridge." It was the least I could do, in my bedbound state.

Although Nina was probably unsure about how to relate to me, seeing me in this sterile place with all the uncertainty that loomed, I appreciated her homely, bright and present attitude.

Three of my OT friends from uni – Tanya, Lizzy and Jenny – soon joined Nina and me in my room, balancing yellow tulips on top of a pizza box.

"Hi Em, feel like some good food?" Jenny asks enthusiastically.

I glance at the untouched pink meal tray. "Yes please."

Tanya leaves to find a jar for the flowers and Jenny and Lizzy sit on either side of my bed. The cardboard pizza box rests on my outstretched splinted leg. A waft of warm yumminess hits me and my appetite kicks in. "You gals are the best." I bite into a piece and, in comfortable silence, we eat the entire contents of the box while it is hot.

~

My other constant visitors were my family. My sister even flew down from Sydney with her husband to share the news that they were going to start trying to have a baby. The prospect of being an auntie for the first time was very exciting, but I had no idea what a huge role nieces and nephews would eventually play in my recovery.

There were some visitors, though, who definitely made it harder for me. My ex-boyfriend visited and, although it was great to see him again, I didn't really want to see him when I was lying in a hospital bed in pyjamas. I'd say that every person in that situation wants their ex to leave thinking, "Man I wish she was still my girlfriend," but I'm sure he left thinking, "I'm so glad Em and I aren't together."

As the weeks went by, physical reasons for my symptoms were being ruled out one by one. Soon the staff began to speculate about the possibility that I had a psychological disorder. I was a young neurological OT who had a lot of visitors and jars full of flowers. Was it that I loved getting the attention? Perhaps I was trying to present like one of my own patients? I was handballed to a psychiatrist who decided I possibly had a 'conversion disorder', which meant that at a subconscious level I was putting this whole thing on.

I was gutted by this latest speculation. *As if I would choose not to run when I loved it so much!* But as the days passed many staff became more convinced that the problem was mental not physical. The idea spread like wildfire and I felt powerless to disprove it, even though I knew it was ridiculous. I realised with growing horror that my ultimate diagnosis was totally out of my control. I was also terrified that this latest psychological diagnosis would distract them from discovering the underlying physical condition that I knew was lurking somewhere in my body.

Meanwhile my non-medical friends tried all tactics to get my leg to work, from massages to attempting to entice my stubborn legs to walk to the café to get more edible food. Friends with medical knowledge, whether they were still studying or practising, tried all the tests they knew but they, like the doctors I saw, failed to diagnose my problem.

Hardest of all was watching my dad, a doctor, silently tick off all the conditions he had learnt and diagnosed. I was so proud of him and had always admired his skills, knowledge base and commitment. He'd always been there to solve any problem I had. In this case, when it mattered so much, he couldn't rescue me. I hated that I was causing both my parents to worry about the danger I was in.

I could no longer walk without assistance and still had a bulky, dark-blue splint strapped to my left leg. Previously, misjudging doorframes and other objects had been easy to cover up, excused as being 'careless'. Now my increasingly warped perception of my body was in the spotlight. At an early physiotherapy session at the Alfred I was sitting on the right side of my bed on a blue vinyl Kingston chair.

"OK, on the count of three, push up on those armrests and stand up tall, Em," the physio instructed.

I rocked my torso from side to side to the seat's edge in preparation.

"OK, one, two ..." she said, supporting my left side.

"Let's do it!" I positioned my hands on the armrests.

I held my breath. I peered down, making sure my feet were positioned side by side. To my horror, only my right foot was in sight – my left foot was still under the chair. Terrified, I collapsed my forearms and retreated into the chair.

"What happened, Em?" she asked.

Unable to stop the tears in my eyes or the shakiness in my voice I looked up towards the physio and said, "My left foot is not where I thought it was."

Weeks into my hospital stay still no one had worked out what was wrong with me. Desperate to get out of the sterile hospital environment, I put in a request for day leave. Even though I had to leave in a wheelchair, I was out of my pyjamas and outside those stark hospital walls. My leg still throbbed and walking was difficult, but the normality of being at my brother's home and being surrounded by non-medical conversation was refreshing.

That afternoon when Dad dropped me back at the hospital I insisted on making my own way to the ward. I was feeling good, self-propelling my wheelchair down the long corridor. For the first time in weeks I thought I could see the light at the end of the tunnel. But as I approached my room a doctor stopped me. "Where have you been?" he demanded. "You shouldn't leave the premises with a tumour in your head."

Suddenly all that surrounded me was darkness, just endless darkness. I had no idea that the results from my latest MRI had come in and I wasn't meant to leave. But much, much worse was hearing the word that had never been mentioned before in all the medical investigations of my condition. 'Tumour!'

I felt so sick at the thought of having something in my head. I pictured a radiating black PacMan-like growth, munching on my healthy brain, engulfing my insides. *Chomp, chomp, chomp*. With each chomp, it was enlarging in size. I held back the tears until the moment I was left alone, then I sobbed uncontrollably. For the first time I wished I had a roommate to talk to. I had a tumour. I had thought my journey being a patient might be coming to an end, but it had only just begun.

Chapter 6
A Diagnosis at Last

As it happened there wasn't a tumour, but the doctors were closing in on the real cause. The weeks of false leads and agonising waiting for a reason were about to end. On the 15th of April, almost three weeks after arriving at the Alfred, I was sent for an angiogram. This is a complicated and invasive procedure but at this stage the doctors were trying anything and everything to find some organic reason for my symptoms.

A cerebral angiogram is a diagnostic test that produces an image of the arteries in the brain. A long thin catheter is threaded through a blood vessel, usually in the upper thigh, all the way up to the head. Once the catheter is in place, the radiologist injects a special dye into the arteries of the brain. Then the image of the brain is taken.

I was told the likelihood of having a stroke during or after the procedure was high, so I had to stay awake. This certainly didn't help my growing anxiety.

"Take this little pill, Sweetie, it'll calm those nerves," the nurse said, handing me a glass of water and a Valium.

Desperate to rid myself of the enormous butterflies colliding in my belly, I grabbed and swallowed the tablet. But no medication would calm me enough or distract my attention from what followed.

I was lying on a plinth-like bench in the middle of a big, darkly lit room. A thin white hospital gown pretended to cover my freezing body. Two masked people hovered over me. "We've numbed the area so you shouldn't feel us inserting the catheter," one of the white coats said before shoving a tube inside my leg. While setting up the equipment he explained, "We will fire the dye into different arteries in your brain and then we'll leave the room and take photos of what we see … Just need you to stay nice and still." This he added before walking out of my sight. I heard his footsteps fading and a door closing.

"No one's going to stay here with me?" Tears welled. The nurse rubbed my right hand reassuringly. "We can't stay with you because of the radiation, but will be just behind that glass window over there." She pointed to the other side of the room.

Replacing her company with another white hospital blanket, she left me alone with my peaking anxiety. *This is torture. I can't handle this.* I lay there listening to the sound of my thumping heart, feeling sandwiched between the hard metal surface I'm lying on and my escalating fear. The eerie silence was soon broken by a crackling noise and a male voice.

"Are you OK Emma? We're all behind the glass window on your right but we'll be talking to you all the time on this microphone."

Trying to turn towards the voice I realise my neck is restrained so instead I whimper an unconvincing 'yep'.

Before I know it, my anxiety engulfs me.

"I'm scared," I call out. I am crying now but I don't care.

"You're OK. Hopefully it won't take too long … now just stay still Emma." He seemed to ignore my fear.

If I had thought all the other procedures I'd been through, from MRIs to nerve-conduction tests, were bad, what followed for the next few hours was off the scale. The agonising process was prolonged each time by a staff member intermittently re-entering the room, repositioning the machine and shooting more dye into my brain. Then they exited the room to take photos behind the window. They'd instruct me over the loudspeaker to, "Breathe … you're doing well," and then, "Now hold still … hold, hold, hold" when taking the images.

Although I managed to stay physically very still, my mind raced. Any chance of human comfort was behind the glass of a distant room. As the dye was released into my arteries to allow them to glimpse the mysteries of the brain the sensations were excruciating. One minute I felt like someone was pouring turps down my throat, the next my head felt like it was on fire.

In the recovery room, a young male doctor removed the catheter and blood spurted everywhere. He applied pressure to the area to stop the bleeding while calling to a nearby nurse, "She won't stop bleeding!" The nurse came over to see if she could assist but accidentally pulled the wrong curtain. As my bed was conveniently positioned under the television, the other patients' eyes were looking in my direction and my leaking body was exposed to the whole room. *Great!* Fifty minutes later they wheeled me, exposed and vulnerable, back to my room. Nauseous from the long procedure and seeing stars, having been stripped of any form of comfort for the entire procedure, I was relieved to see my close family and friends waiting in my room.

The morning after the angiogram another doctor entered my room, introducing himself with a comforting handshake. "Mr John McMahon. I'm a neurosurgeon here at the Alfred." He sat on the visitor chair next to my bed. After a brief chat about the weather, we skipped the small talk. "So I looked at the angiogram, which shows that you have an arteriovenous malformation [AVM], or knot of blood vessels, in your brainstem," he said.

A diagnosis? At last?

"Is that bad … What is it?" I sat upright.

"An AVM is a congenital condition, so you're born with it. It's a bit like a birthmark but in the brain. It's comprised of a tangle of blood vessels. In most cases these untangle as you develop but yours have remained knotted." He demonstrated the tangle of blood vessels by clasping his hands together, interlacing his fingers and twisting his wrists in opposite directions, then went on to explain that the angiogram also showed that it had bled once recently and once in the past. "The dehydration associated with your climb up Mt Kinabalu may have precipitated the recent bleed and onset of symptoms, resulting in your left-sided paralysis," he said.

Apparently the earlier MRI scans failed to pick up the AVM because it was in the brainstem, which is surrounded by bone. The devastating news was that my AVM was like a time bomb, likely to burst at any moment, and needed to be removed.

"We'll chat about this with your parents, Emma. Don't worry. You're in good hands here." He put his hand on my right shoulder reassuringly and smiled compassionately before turning around and leaving my room.

I felt overwhelmed, but also relieved that there was a physiological reason to explain everything. *I did have something physically wrong with me.* All the support and love I had received from family and friends now seemed deserved. I had been under immense strain, feeling terribly guilty when no one could work out what was wrong with me. At the same time I felt completely exhausted, depleted by weeks of worrying – worn down and no longer able to convince them that there was an organic reason for my predicament.

After feeling handballed between so many different specialists who seemed to struggle with juggling their intellect and bedside manner, meeting Mr McMahon renewed my faith in the medical profession. He was extremely intelligent and had been honest but also tactful in relaying difficult news. I was thankful that it was he who finally told me what was wrong. But I was left with a zillion thoughts and questions I hadn't asked. *This AVM thing has always been in my head. It's bled. How much? It's going to explode. When? How will they remove it? Is it dangerous?*

After the AVM was found, I was moved to the neurology ward. They wheeled me to a room that I was to share with a lady who had had a stroke. She spoke little English, and continually stripped and made her bed, and thought I was a bank teller. She would wake up in the middle of the night screaming gibberish.

Another patient did laps of the ward, clutching a handbag closely and wearing a permanent grin, as if she'd just been told she'd won a million dollars. She seemed to suffer from short-term memory loss. She introduced herself three times in the first ten minutes.

In my role as a neuro OT I had often worked with patients like this, but never imagined I would one day be there among them. I felt frightened and alone. I remembered then that the last patient I'd had before I was suddenly admitted also had an AVM. She had suffered a stroke as a result. At the time I had only really been focusing on her stroke. Now I could only think about my AVM. The AVM in my head.

Chapter 7
More to Prove

The next logical stop was the serious task of discussing what to do about the AVM, but it seemed I still had more to prove. Unbelievably, despite now having a physical diagnosis, the next day the previously scheduled psychiatric assessment still went ahead. I understood that the doctor was being holistic in his approach, but I did find this hard to comprehend. *Surely I had enough to contend with?* I feared that any resistance to being assessed would only nourish their doubts about me. So I went to my scheduled appointment without any argument.

~

The room is small, dark and musty. A naked cork pin-board hangs crookedly on the far wall. The senior psychiatrist sits opposite me in a white coat, his name badge a constant reminder of his status. He has coarse grey hair and his skin is wrinkled like an acorn. He leans back in the soft armchair in a relaxed manner and crosses his right leg over his left knee in an open, figure-four position. I do feel intimidated but don't want to let his confident manner get to me. *Be brave, you have nothing to hide.*

A younger colleague wearing a light-blue polo shirt sits upright on a wooden chair in the corner of the tiny room, quietly observing. There seems to be a real hierarchy here.

The psychiatrist begins scanning my sexual history, asking if I had ever been abused as a child. Despite determining that I had nothing but an amazing childhood, later in the interview he reverts to this topic. He leans forward so his forearms are resting on his thighs and whispers slowly and clearly, "Do you orgasm a lot?" and "Do you like it hard?"

My eyes widen in disbelief. I gulp. *Is he serious?* These are just two of the questions posed by him in this tortuous assessment. Inwardly I am furious, but I don't want his inappropriate questions to intimidate me. His eyes penetrate as my mind searches for the right response. *How does he want me to reply? What is the right answer?*

After that interrogation the best he could come up with was that I was anxious and depressed, and he prescribed me anti-depressants. His written diagnosis admitted there was some organic cause for my illness but that it was exacerbated by psychological factors. He thought that I might be reacting psychologically to my twin sister's and mother's serious illnesses a few years earlier, speculating that I might be suffering from 'survivor guilt'. He added 'possible conversion disorder' to my medical file.

I couldn't believe he would sit there with a young woman going through the trauma of a real-life time bomb in the brain and just narrowly look for a psychological answer. I was shocked that he would offer a diagnosis of depression without considering *why* I might be depressed. My experience in that consultation only made me more sceptical about those 'caring' for me. I felt that my responses had to be tailored to what he wanted to hear. He had failed to even try to understand my true state of mind. If I had already been anxious and depressed, it became much worse after this insensitive consultation, even though I never resorted to his prescribed anti-depressants.

It was a relief when a couple of weeks later I finally got an appointment at the AVM clinic. With a serious condition like the one I now knew I had, it is standard medical practice to get all the different specialists together in a room to discuss treatment options. I went along with Dad to the William Buckland Centre at the Alfred. By this time I had heard many different opinions on what could be done about the AVM. I knew this was my chance to consolidate all the different techniques and make a decision.

I enter the dark and sombre meeting room. An image of my brain is enlarged on the wall and a group of white-coated doctors sit around a massive circular wooden table. I soon learn that there are two neurosurgeons, one neuro-radiologist and one radiotherapist. I sit nervously next to my dad. Thankfully I'm sandwiched between him and Mr John McMahon, two people I trust. The other neurosurgeon, dressed in operating scrubs, perches on a chair next to Dad, committing neither to sitting nor standing, holding my bulging medical file in one hand, his mobile in the other.

In turn each professional gives his opinion regarding treating the monster featured in the image behind me, the convoluted knot of blood vessels that is my AVM. I listen attentively, squinting and straining to catch their mumbling words, searching desperately for any optimistic word like 'hope' or 'recovery'. I have brought a dictaphone in my bag, but I don't dare ask to record the discussion. I am already intimidated enough by them. When I studied OT we had been taught the importance of 'client-centred' practice and communicating with patients as equals. Most of the doctors in this room either don't want to be bogged down with that seemingly simple stuff, or they missed the lecture on client-centredness.

They seem to barely notice I am there. I am sitting in front of the enormous image of my own brain, and the deadly AVM inside it, while they talk to each other, almost excitedly, about the severity of the problem. It's good to have Dad by my side, a doctor who can speak their language. He is also my advocate and is as horrified as I am by the real implications of the image on the wall. Thankfully, he is able to challenge this room full of experts to explain themselves clearly.

The first possibility, we hear, is just to leave the AVM alone and monitor it. But the angiogram showed it had recently leaked and they agree there is a high chance that it will bleed again in the near future. In fact, there's a 50 per cent chance of it bleeding again over the next 30 years. They all decide, without even a glance in my direction, that leaving it is not an option.

The neuro-radiologist discusses *embolising* the AVM. This involves injecting superglue into it to block the vessels. But in my case, the AVM has too many vessels connected to the surrounding vital brain tissue. So there is the danger of 'collateral damage' – other blood vessels and surrounding brain tissue being destroyed. I watch the neuro-radiologist as he sits in the corner with a remote, flipping through the various slides of the different cross-sections of my brain, seemingly removed from the discussion. It is clear he doesn't think embolisation is an option. He doesn't want to treat me.

Then it is the radiotherapist's turn. He says my AVM can be treated with radiotherapy as a day procedure. This sounds less invasive, but leaves a high risk that it could bleed again in the near future. He warns me that the surrounding brain could also be impacted by this treatment. Apparently my AVM is sandwiched between cranial nerve V, responsible for facial sensation, and nerve V11, enabling facial movement.

"You could lose the ability to blink or sense when you have foreign material, like dirt in your eyes. Also, visual problems such as corneal ulcers and double vision could result," he says grimly. "If certain nerves were damaged it could result in facial pain," he adds. I force myself to nod. I appreciate his honesty. I have no idea that *all* the things he talks about, and more, are ahead of me.

Then it is the turn of the neurosurgeons. Mr McMahon explains that he feels surgery is the best option, adding that I would have to spend time in rehab first, as they wouldn't want to operate on something that had freshly bled. Also my chances of a quick recovery would be increased if I could learn to walk independently again. Using his fingers to trace lines on my head, he quickly shows what they'd do if I went ahead with the surgery. "We'd make an incision behind your right ear, then remove part of your skull bone to get to the AVM. Then we'd just clip it, remove it, replace the bone and then stitch you all up again."

It sounds simple. I feel hopeful. This relief is short-lived when the other more experienced neurosurgeon interrupts, saying, "I wouldn't touch her with a ten-foot pole!"

My heart sinks. Apparently, the chance of me dying during the operation is too high. I glance at Dad desperately to see if I've heard the words correctly. Dad puts his hand on my right knee. My advocate has surrendered. I thought listening to such disagreement between experts in the field would give me clarity. But I am feeling more frightened and more confused.

At the same time I am boiling with anger and frustration. I had been sitting for what seems like hours in this dark room with a group of experts talking about my brain in an abstract scientific fashion. They seem oblivious that the patient they are speaking or arguing about is in the same room. It's my life and my death that they are discussing. Worse, they still haven't come up with a definite solution. My AVM and I now seem dismissed and they can turn their attention to the next case. The sound of rustling papers, clicking pens and the dragging of chairs tell me the meeting is over as far as they are concerned. A waft of cold air enters the room as one doctor leaves.

But I'm not ready to leave yet. My AVM is still ticking away. This is my only chance to get at least some useful information from them. I quickly blurt out some questions I'd scribbled down earlier.

"Can I fly?"

"Can I drink alcohol?"

"How long would it be before I return to work and running?"

I feel stupid asking these now, after the seriousness of what I just heard. Desperate, I do anyway. It is pitch dark in the room. Thankfully, I can't see their rolling eyes or smirking expressions, but I soon know I've lost their attention. After asking a couple of questions my voice fades as I realise no one is listening. The harsh fluoro lights flick on. They quickly leave the room.

I limp after them, feeling physically and emotionally helpless. Stranded. Desolate.

I guess I expected to leave with a solution of sorts and a treatment date. Instead, I seem to have ignited a lot of medical argument. No one is willing to take the risk to separate me from the ticking time bomb in my head.

Speechless, Dad and I enter the lift. There is nothing to say, and my thoughts are spiralling downwards. Mr McMahon catches the doors as they are closing and squeezes inside the metal box to join us. The three of us stand in awkward silence. I can tell Mr McMahon is in deep thought. My AVM ticks, Dad's frustration brews and McMahon's conscience surfaces. As we all exit the lift, Mr McMahon suddenly turns around to face us as if he's made a decision.

He says, "I am going to swallow my pride and suggest that you, Emma, seek the expertise of my very experienced teacher and colleague in Sydney, Professor Michael Morgan." He seems relieved at his escaping words. He adds that although he would learn so much by operating on me, he knows that if I were his own daughter he'd let Professor Morgan operate. My respect for him, already high, is now off the scale. Even though I have no definite plan, at least I am left with some possibility.

Although there was some clarity, I was still left with the agonising decision of whether or not to risk the surgery. Radiotherapy and embolism were clearly not options because both left the chance of the AVM rupturing in the near future. If that happened the outcome would be fatal. I felt too young to be taking on such a responsibility. For 24 years the hardest decision I had ever had to make was choosing between chocolate, strawberry or vanilla ice-cream and yet here I was having to decide whether to have life-threatening brain surgery. It was so tempting to take the chance, ignore the AVM, return to my old life and plan to one day get married and have children.

But I knew that if I went on living with the threat of sudden death hanging over me, it would hugely affect my life and all my future relationships. After hours and days deliberating with my doctors, family and friends I decided to have brain surgery. It was that or drop dead.

Chapter 8
The Therapist Becomes the Patient

Once the decision was made I couldn't wait to get this thing ripped out of my head. But my AVM and I had been together for 24 years, and we were going to be forced to spend yet more time together. Ironically, before I could have surgery I had to learn to walk again, so I was transferred by ambulance to Caulfield General Medical Centre where I had worked as an OT two years earlier. Now I was about to see it from the other side.

With me in the ambulance was a man in his mid fifties who had had a stroke. He was paralysed down his left side, had a facial droop and couldn't speak clearly. I could tell he was anxious when he introduced himself, "I am John and it's difficult to understand me." Actually I *could* understand him. Many of my former patients had similar speech difficulties. For the first time I could see a positive side to my situation. I was still a therapist and could reassure him, but at the same time rapport was much easier to build because I felt at his level. I was now a patient too. We'd both been struck down by a neurological condition and were both approaching unknown territory.

In that bleak time it was a small comforting thought, that I was now a powerful combination of patient and therapist.

But this positive frame of mind was soon challenged when the ambulance entered the gates of Caulfield Hospital. I spotted a white station wagon with a familiar number plate, SPY 923. It was a hospital car I had once driven. I also recognised the OT behind the wheel and I was suddenly painfully aware of my change in role. That first night I wrote in my diary:

I entered Rehab 2 overwhelmed. I was tired. A single room was a relief. I was wheeled past a social worker I had worked with. I wanted to hide, but sitting there in my frilly pyjamas unable to walk I was forced to acknowledge her. Puzzled she said, "I know you from somewhere?" I was exposed. My disguise was blown. I reluctantly said, "I worked with you."

My colleagues were also confused by their own role in my rehabilitation. Upon my arrival, a handwritten note was left on my bed on top of a pile of neatly folded clothes for me to borrow.

Hey Em, Hope your first night is OK … I've got a feeling you might be inundated by work people … so will let you get into a routine and look forward to spending some time with you on the weekend. I'm thinking of you always, though, and am here if you need me. Love you lots – have a good day and keep smiling!

These words were just a small slice of the constant love, support and encouragement I received throughout my rehab. But in spite of all that, I became steadily more depressed and anxious. I hated my former colleagues seeing me around the clock. They saw my low points and my tears and attended to all my needs, even changed my bedpan. And what worried me most was their access to my medical history, where they would see the query of a 'psychological condition' stamped on my file. Even though my condition was diagnosed as a physical one, I was still haunted by the words of the psychiatrist at the Alfred.

I knew I should be concentrating on getting physically better but I was torn between dealing with the AVM diagnosis, grappling with my decision to have a craniotomy and accepting the loss of independence, dignity and self-worth. Yet I wanted to be brave for my family and for my colleagues.

Day by day my anxiety about the time bomb in my head grew. I didn't know what the warning signs of my AVM rupturing would be. All I was told was that I couldn't increase my heart rate, hold my breath or lift anything too heavy. Any strange feeling in my head panicked me. I'd buzz, the nurse would respond and take my pulse and blood pressure … I was driving the staff crazy. I'd wake every morning and do an exaggerated smile to make sure my AVM hadn't ruptured during the night.

I lie on my bed, wide awake, but with my eyes shut to deter my roommate from chattering non-stop about her problems. I want to be alone, to get some time out from this hell before Louise, my friend from work, arrives. But shutting my eyes doesn't shut out my AVM. It talks to me in an urgent pulsating tone. It seems to enlarge and louden with each second and the more attention I give it, the bigger and more lethal it becomes. *Focus on another sensation*. I remind myself to breathe. Apparently regular oxygen flow will tame my AVM, prevent it from blowing. Lou's here any minute. I wish I'd cancelled. *How do I act in front of her? Do I keep pretending things are dandy for my visitors' sake? Surely if*

I make it hard for them, I'll push them away and they won't get hurt. I can let them escape.

Footsteps enter the room and my eyes open.

"Hey there, Emmy." Louise walks towards me.

"Hi," I say, avoiding too much eye contact. I have to concentrate on staying in a grumpy mood and not let her snap me out of my negative mindset.

"Can I sit?" she asks, lowering herself into my visitor chair. It hisses, letting out trapped air from the cracked, brown vinyl surface and breaking the awkward silence I'm deliberately creating. I stay on top of my white bed covers, hugging my bent right leg close to my chest and leaving my stubborn left leg outstretched. I rest my right ear on my knee. My white Ted (compression) stockings look hideous under my grey trackies.

"So how's things, Em? You don't seem too happy today."

A tear escapes down my check. I quickly wipe it away on my sleeve before she notices.

"I'm OK," I lie.

"So … um … What have you done today?"

"Not much," I say, in a monotonous tone.

Silence. Awkward silence. Silence that I would normally fill.

"Oh … um … Well, work's quite busy. Jasmine's gone away so I've taken on her caseload for a bit. Everyone at work says hi, by the way."

I grin briefly, resuming a sombre and blank expression. *Poor thing, she's trying and I hate seeing her struggle to cheer me up.* I consider pretending I'm OK for her sake.

"The funniest thing … So Miranda was on her lunch break and … "

I find myself not listening to her story. *Nothing's funny anymore. Miranda hasn't even contacted me since this all happened. Besides, lunch here is gross.*

She laughs. It's contagious and I find myself laughing along. It feels good. She's broken the self-pity spell.

Lou glances awkwardly at her watch, saying, "I'll get a parking fine so have to go now, Em!"

The nurse enters to take my blood pressure. Relief replaces my anxiety for a moment.

Lou occupies herself on her phone while the nurse pulls up my right sleeve and wraps the blue cuff around my arm. I watch the nurse look at the rising dial and my anxiety inwardly escalates. When she scribbles down the result on the clipboard, I'm relieved to hear that my blood pressure is normal. I collapse my tense body back onto the pillow behind me. *I can relax until the next check.*

The nurse removes the cuff from my arm, puts the pen back in her scruffy hair-do and exits the room, wheeling the machine behind her.

Lou looks up, saying, "All done?"

"Sorry, Lou Lou," I quickly blurt out.

"It's fine, I had to text Jane about tonight's netball game anyway."

"No, I mean sorry for my grumpy mood. I'm not in a good way, I hate being in here." I'm crying now.

She rises from her chair and hugs me tightly. I let her, folding into her and hugging her back.

"I know, Em, understand totally. It's crap. The whole situation is crap, you don't deserve this!" She pulls back from the embrace, stares directly into my teary red eyes, clutches my shoulders and almost shakes me back and forth to reinforce her statement.

"It's all good though," I perk up, reaching for a tissue and blowing my nose.

"It's *not* 'all good', Em ... I have to go but I'll visit again soon, OK? And will text soon." Again, she hugs me tightly and then stands up, turning while grabbing her bag and walks towards the door.

"Thanks for cheering me up Lou," I say behind her.

She blows a kiss from the doorway and leaves.

Another thing preoccupying me at that time was my love life – or lack of it. As a young girl who had previously been in several long-standing relationships, I had never envisaged a future without a partner. Now I felt intensely lonely and wished I could share what I was going through with a significant other.

I wrote in my diary:

A guy I had met a few weeks before this hell ride has been texting and calling. I ignored his messages initially but knowing I won't be in a position to see him again in the near future I just texted him. I felt I needed to justify my sudden disappearance. All I wrote was, "Running injury turned out worse than thought." I was honest. I just deliberately omitted A LOT of the other information. A girl with a time bomb in her brain is hardly attractive. I am now high maintenance, whether I want to be or not.

The waiting period at Caulfield was the hardest time of all. I often only had one hour of therapy a day, so I had way too much time to think about my future. During the day my friends and colleagues were working. In the evenings their visits were comforting but by then I had had the entire day to stew. Often I felt closed to their attempts to infect me with their positivity, and unable to celebrate their good news. Friends who had previously told me their problems suddenly stopped sharing, reluctant to dwell on their issues, which now they probably thought were minuscule in comparison to mine. I felt as though I was tainting everyone's lives.

I was definitely heading into a downward spiral, having become inward focused and self-indulged, bitter, irritable and resentful. Rather than leaning on the amazing supports I had, afraid of impacting their lives more than I had already since my admission, I chose to shut them out.

Eventually I knew I needed to return home for my own mental wellbeing. All too soon I would have to re-enter the sterile hospital realm for my craniotomy. My therapy team were reluctant to let me leave. From their perspectives I was still making physical gains. But they understood my rationale that I had to remain emotionally fit as well. More time inside the rehab walls was going to destroy any remaining sanity I might have.

Chapter 9
A Brief Taste of Independence

Once I knew I could leave rehabilitation, all I could think about was returning to my old life. But it wasn't that simple. My Richmond pad had stairs, and my operation wasn't until June. It was only mid-April and I didn't have enough money to pay rent for that long. I reluctantly agreed to move back to my parents' ground-level, more accessible home where they could care for me. But moving back was an emotional whirlwind I wasn't prepared for. Everything had changed.

Mum wheeled me into my rental unit and my housemate greeted us. It seemed like yesterday that I'd complained to him about my body falling apart. Now here I was in a wheelchair, level with his bellybutton. I didn't chat to him for long, as I was on a mission to reclaim my personal belongings before the entire family removalist party arrived. Before Mum had closed the front door I was out of my wheel chair and bum-dragging reverse style up the 26 steps to my room. Mum got there before me, boxes in hand. I burst into tears. Like any girl my age there were things I really would rather my mother didn't see, but there was no way I could be private about this. She was there to help and I had to grin and bear it. Thankfully, my twin sister soon arrived and was able to pack one box full of personal things so I could try to keep some dignity.

What followed was like a tornado hitting. In one hour everything was packed, the removalists were sweaty and hungry. I felt practically hurled back into my wheelchair and into the car and we drove away, that part of my life gone. I was angry. Thoughts flew around, colliding violently inside my head. *What if I could manage those stairs?* I was sure I'd be back walking soon. But whether I improved or not, with my upcoming craniotomy and the dependent state I'd be in afterwards, I knew in my heart that I couldn't live there anymore.

Installed in my new home, I later wrote in my diary:

I'm in my wheelchair and have been plonked in my parents' lounge room. I can hear chatter and laughter in the next room. But I want to be alone. No time for farewells, my belongings were boxed or given away ... I feel trapped – they may as well have gaffa taped me up in one of those twelve boxes.

In spite of my restlessness at being home with Mum and Dad, I did gradually begin to make physical gains. My left side was becoming stronger. I could soon walk independently with a single-point stick and only needed my wheelchair for long distances. As I improved physically I began to question my decision to undergo brain surgery. *Why had I chosen to go through such a dangerous operation? Why remove something so tiny now, when it has been with me for 24 years?* In a few weeks I'd be walking normally, and the possibility of just returning to my previous life was tantalising. But I knew that masking the problem would only prolong any suffering and I couldn't live with this time bomb ticking in my head.

While I waited for my operation, I spent my days shopping, seeing friends and going to the gym … Preparing. Definitely distracting myself. I caught up with the people who were important to me. Everyone said, "Just see it as a holiday. Make the most of it." *Sure,* I thought, *how do you make the most of your life when it's about to end?*

Since Bec and I were identical twins, she also had to undergo a brain scan to ascertain whether she had an AVM. The days leading up to this procedure and awaiting the results were torture. Bec and I have always dealt with stressors very differently. While I internalise my anxieties, Bec verbalises hers. She agonised constantly. "What do I do if I have a VCR (Bec's attempt at using the 'AVM' medical jargon) in my head?" "What if …?"

Everything she said, including "My head feels weird!" mirrored my thinking. But I *had* been indisputably diagnosed with this time bomb, while whether she had one or not was still unknown. Her nervous questions were totally understandable but I would exit the room and cry to myself quietly. I felt responsible for her distress and the prospect of my parents having to care for *two* disabled adults in the future was terrifying.

Thankfully Bec's brain scan results were clear and she exited relieved. Despite feeling immensely guilty about being the one that was OK, she was quite chuffed that the scan revealed that her brain was quite big! In fact, according to my Dad, her parting question to my surgeon was, "Is my brain bigger than Em's?" Although I was so grateful for her result, I secretly hated that it was now my AVM diagnosis that differentiated us as twins. *Wasn't it enough that months before she had dyed her hair brown?*

CHAPTER 10
A Date for the Big Day

On the 1st of June 2005, Dad and I flew to Sydney to see Professor Michael Morgan. He was one of the world's most experienced surgeons in this procedure. Hopefully he would be prepared to operate on me. Feeling tired and anxious, we sat in silence waiting for *the man that could save my life* to see us … I was cold, freezing. I didn't know if it was the temperature or the nerves. We both knew that this was the last option. I whispered to Dad, "I hope he agrees to operate." He just nodded into his chest.

Entering Professor Morgan's spacious room, me limping behind Dad on my stick, I plonk down in the vacant chair. As my AVM pulsates Professor Morgan looks over the scan results he's received from Melbourne. I see his serious expression and his moving lips as he speaks, but I subconsciously block out all sound. I'm relying on Dad to listen and summarise the conversation later. I stare at the presentation, the stats and columns labelled DEAD versus RECOVERED. I don't ask about the likelihood of paralysis. It seems irrelevant. I'd be stupid if I believed he knew. He doesn't. No one knows.

I sat in that cold room with two men, focusing on trapping the tears trying to escape down my face. In desperation I looked around for a tissue. Dad noticed and patted my shoulder with a deeply concerned look. Professor Morgan said, "We will look after you," and passed me the tissue box next to the plastic brain on his desk.

My tears eventually did escape when he told us that the cost of the procedure would be more than $100,000. This fee included the operation, doctors and private hospital fees. As my case was urgent, it was too risky to wait for a bed in a public hospital. But without private health insurance how would I pay for it? I already owed my parents $4000 for my Africa trip. That was nothing compared to this. There were so many things I would have preferred to spend the money on, like a massive deposit on a house or hundreds of holidays. Instead, I was opting to spend 100 grand to have my head carved, bone drilled and my tiny AVM removed and clipped; an operation likely to leave me dead or with all sorts of deficits like deafness and muscle weakness. Perhaps a wise but dubious investment!

Professor Morgan explained that they would have to mobilise the temporal lobe of my brain so they could move it out of the way to get to the AVM. Seizures could result, though they would initially put me on anti-convulsants to prevent these. This medication might affect my menstrual cycle post-surgery, along with my ability to get pregnant in the future.

How different I felt after that consultation. It took just one hour for all other options to be definitely ruled out. The operation was the only procedure left. *If* had been replaced with *when* and *how much* and *where*. I was on a one-way path and there was no going back. I was petrified.

We left his room and went to the reception counter. "Hi Emma, so you'd like to make a time for your craniotomy with

Professor Morgan here in Sydney?"

I forced a nod. She looked at her computer screen. I watched her manicured fingers scroll the mouse. They stopped moving. "OK let's see … our next available time is on the 17th of June 2005. How would that suit?"

I wanted to say, "Let me just check my diary." Instead I whimpered, "That would be … fine." Then I found myself sobbing uncontrollably. I could no longer stand upright. My stick seemed to buckle under me. I resorted to draping my exhausted, helpless body over the dark wooden counter. Dad seemed to pick me up by simultaneously squeezing both my shoulders reassuringly. I turned to him and wept into his checked sports jacket.

"It's OK, Love, good that we have a date now." He patted my back and assured me that I had made the right decision.

I didn't give the receptionist eye contact again, fearing I'd only cry. Dad guided me to the lift and we left in silence.

CHAPTER 11
So This Is Goodbye

Back in Melbourne I had less than a week to farewell my old life and plan what I could for the immediate future. My *one-way* flight to Sydney was booked for the 16th of June.

Even though I thought it was unnecessary (I was young, I wasn't going to die!), I took my parents' advice and organised to meet with a solicitor and sign my will. While friends were signing their credit cards for their latest purchases, I was autographing my will. My dad and brother now had medical power of attorney. To my parents I just signed over my debt in the case of my death. "Surely, when I die I want to leave something good," I thought sadly.

That done, I was determined to appreciate the days I had left. My closest friends organised a trip to my family's beach house in Anglesea. They say salty sea air heals wounds, so I secretly hoped it would fix me and, if not, give me the clarity and distance I needed to get things into perspective.

On that weekend we girls went everywhere together, our elbows linked. I was scared, terrified to let go. The mood between us was subdued. We'd exchange anxious glances and our eyes were often filled with tears. We tried to distract each other with anecdotes, but they seemed minor considering I was about to be cut away from the group.

For that entire time by the sea I inwardly paced, wondering if it was my last 'girl holiday'. You suddenly appreciate everything so much more when you realise it may vanish soon.

I had knitted each of my friends a scarf and attached the following note:

Warm hugs
I've wrapped my hugs within this scarf
To bring you warmth when things go wrong
And to bring you sunshine on winter days
As well as to thank you for your caring ways
In each row I have stitched in a smile
It's here for you mile after mile
As we walk together or walk alone
My cheerful thoughts are yours to own
So wear this scarf, full of special things
And remember me and all that our friendship brings
The knitting's not great – there's a hole or two
But it comes with warm hugs from me to you
Love always
Em

For every family member I bought a present to help them remember me. Unlike my Christmas impulse buys, suddenly I had to think of something that encompassed my whole relationship with each person. I chose items that could be engraved with a personal message. For Dad and Pete a silver key ring, for Mum a locket, for Bec a bracelet and for Kate a necklace.

I was surprised when Bec gave me a canvas print she had designed and painted, based on a childhood photo of us with a wheelbarrow of home-grown apples. The words, *Two halves make a whole*, were etched across it. For the first time it really hit me that this wasn't a thing that would just rock *my* life. I would be missed.

On the night of the 14th of June I had a casual dinner at my parents' home. This was my last opportunity to thank people and to say goodbye. I knew how risky the procedure was going to be and that if I did survive the operation things would be very different. My family knew the seriousness of my situation but I hadn't told my friends and acquaintances.

I wrote in my diary:

People were coming over for dinner – neighbours, netball friends, family friends, friends I'd rented with, school friends, work friends, everyone in my life. The room was filled with people. Sitting, standing, squatting people. I felt so lucky to have all this support. It was raining outside but the number of people and the open fire soon generated enough heat. The night rushed by in a blur. I would end one conversation and start another. I hadn't even spoken to half of the people there and then the next minute I'm hugging them goodbye. It was too speedy. But I guess even if I'd had all the time in the world it would've been hard. What's time, when time feels like it's ending anyway? I think it was hard for everyone to understand how serious this is. Many hadn't seen me since my diagnosis and although I'm walking with a stick, I'm probably looking better than I have for a while. The night was finished. Silence. Eerie silence. The people I cared about had now left. It felt like just me and the leftover peppermint slice.

After that I had only 24 hours left as 'Em' before surgery. There was no time to waste. Every second seemed vital.

Chapter 12
The Quiet Before the Storm

I arrived at Dalcross Private Hospital in Sydney on the afternoon of the 16th of June 2005. I walked up the driveway from the car park with Mum, Dad and Bec at my side. Dalcross wasn't big and cold like many of the hospitals I'd seen. It was an old house surrounded by manicured gardens. Inside it was even better; green carpet, modern chairs and walls lined with light oak wood. Dalcross didn't have the same disinfectant odour I associated with hospitals.

I was shown to a nicely carpeted room, my own 'pre-op' preparation space. Vases rather than the typical old jars sat on the oak shelves. A TV hung from the ceiling over my bed-end. The lighting was dim, so much better than the normal hospital fluoro lights that spotlight every blemish.

That afternoon was long. In between the routine blood samples and CT scans my family and I sat in that room and waited. I was tired but too anxious to rest. I felt sick.

"The surgeon will be with you shortly", the nurse said, popping her head around the corner.

What seemed like hours later Professor Morgan entered wearing his scrubs and a mask draped scarf-like around his neck. He removed his blue shower cap and went about shaking everyone's hand. All I could think was, *These hands will be inside my head in about 17 hours.* I returned his grasp softly, and silently hoped my family would do the same, keeping those fingers intact for my operation.

"How was your trip?'" he asked.

"OK, you know, I guess travelling for neurosurgery isn't that riveting." I was keen to skip the small talk and get right to the point.

"I guess not," he said, shaking Mum's hand.

He went on to explain he was having a break from another operation. *This is a break?* I quickly glanced at Mum, who I knew was thinking the same thing.

"I was thinking during my last procedure, instead of accessing your brainstem through your forehead, we'd go behind your ear. There's less chance of seizures and frontal lobe damage that way," he said, drawing an imaginary line on my skull with his finger.

His reasoning made sense but my thoughts boomeranged back to his initial words: "I was thinking during another operation …" Inwardly I panicked. *Surely he should be not thinking about my skull while he's operating on someone else? Does that mean he'll be contemplating other patients' procedures when cutting into my head? When he's operating on my skull I want his 100 per cent attention!*

"Whatever you think's best," I said. He made it sound so simple. *It isn't a haircut – my brain won't grow back.*

"What time will it be? Will I have to shave my head?" I asked anxiously. I had kept my endless worries locked up but they were now seeping out. "Around 8.30am," he said, casually like we were doing coffee. I want an exact time.

"That early? Sure you don't want a strong coffee fix first?" I wanted him to have a good sleep and a relaxed brekky. *What if he had a bad sleep?* There were so many silly things I wanted to ask … *What if he needed to go to the toilet? Would there be meal breaks?*

"It's up to you if you want to shave your whole head or I'll get the nurse to shave behind your right ear," he said.

"I'd just shave your whole head," blurted the nurse taking notes. "Easier to manage after the op and then you're not lop sided."

I wanted to save my hair. I wanted to return to Melbourne as intact as possible. Besides, having a bald head would only make me look sicker.

My escalating fear was only heightened when he introduced his co-surgeon.

"I'll be assisted by my wife, Elizabeth Ritson, during the op," he said, stepping to his left and straightening his right arm like a boom gate, introducing her. She was tall. I noticed her fine glasses and thick hair. *She needed glasses?* I'd been glad my surgeon was bald, no hair to moult. *Great. And what if they had a domestic during the operation.*

My imagination went into overdrive: "Could you please pass me the scalpel," Prof Morgan might say, holding out his empty right rubber-gloved hand.

"No I won't," his wife would reply stubbornly.

"Please Darling, Emma's bleeding," he'd say, his eyes pleading.

"What do I get if I do?" she'd say in a teasing tone.

"Come on, Honey," he'd say more seriously. He'd had enough.

I just hoped my head wouldn't cop the blame for an unironed shirt or a late meeting.

"Well, have a good sleep and we'll see you tomorrow," he said, clicking the folder onto the end of my white bed and walking towards the door. "I've prescribed some relaxants for you before the operation, just to calm those nerves."

"Any for us?" Mum called behind him, trying to joke but I knew she was serious.

He left. I felt as though my head would explode. The AVM and the unanswered questions were smashing around in my skull like dodgem cars.

Later the radiographer wheeled me into his glass-boxed room overlooking the CT white tube that I'd been in earlier when they snapped images of my brain. He showed me the 3D images on his desktop screen. Instead of planning the incisions they'd make by marking lines directly onto my face, they would refer to the bony landmarks on the images of my skull.

"Isn't technology great." He spun the image around by rotating the mouse enthusiastically.

"Yeah." I tried to sound equally excited, but knew too well that the clay-rotating image was my head. *What if they entered into the wrong patient file? Clay could be remoulded but my head could not.*

"You better get some sleep, Dear. You have a big day tomorrow," the nurse said from my doorway.

It was late ... the night before my operation. I didn't want Bec to go. We were watching *Anne of Green Gables* and it hadn't finished. Anne was still stressing about her red hair. I thought about tomorrow's scheduled semi crew cut. I wasn't tired.

Before Bec left that night I quickly wrote on a scrap of paper, "In the case of death, I, Emma Elizabeth Gee, will donate all my organs." Bec witnessed it. It was the last thing I wrote before the sleeping tablet finally took effect.

~

"Wakey wakey, Emma." A chirpy nurse entered, holding some folded blue and white garments under her right arm and a towel in the other hand. "How did you sleep?" She pulled my curtains open.

I sat upright, but before I could answer she told me to dress in the folded items on the end of my bed. "When you're ready, get into this, Dear, and take out any earrings. Just leave your things there and I'll put them in your room for when you wake up."

She left, shutting the door loudly behind her. I had 60 minutes until my family arrived. Sitting up slowly I stared at the items of clothing the nurse had left on the end of my bed, my right hand resting apprehensively on top of them. Blue plastic, pull-up knickers; a blue shower cap and a white sheet-like gown. Usually for big life events like your wedding or birthday you dress up. Instead I get to wear these, and have my head shaved.

I decided to dress, get it over and done with. I wrapped the shapeless one-size-fits-all gown around and clasped and scrunched it closed behind me with both hands till I could feel no breeze. I looked in the mirror. *Hardly flattering. Here we go!* I took my pasty body cocooned in this white tent back to my bed and wrote to kill time.

5.59am …

Dear Diary, Today is the day. It's finally here. I'm sitting in bed as ready as I can be. My back is cold, the stale hospital air is touching my bare skin where the gown parts. I'm terrified, but positive ... I just want to get this over with. The AVM is primed and ticking, ready to explode. I'm thankful it hasn't blown yet. No longer do I have to anxiously wait for it to erupt. In a few hours it will be gone and I will be asleep. Whether I wake or not, I'll be free from this time bomb that's haunted me over the last few months.

6.20am ...
Dear Diary, I feel like I'm waiting for a death sentence. But I'm going to live. I am going to turn frowns into smiles. I am determined to help people like I never have. I am going to get the chance to reciprocate all my family and friends' amazing support.

I closed my diary and put it on my bedside table then sandwiched myself between the stale sheets. I lay like a corpse, stiff and cold. I closed my eyes, reminding myself that today's the day that I have been waiting for.

I didn't hear my family enter the room. Normally I could hear Mum's voice a block away, but even she was speechless. They entered slowly, the quiet before the storm. We were all dreading that day.

My body was frozen cold. Stiff with fear. I turned to face them and opened my eyes, finally letting my tears escape. Bec entered first. Mum, Dad and Kate followed close behind.

"Hey Em," Bec said, unusually softly, tears rising but her pitch remaining flat. Mum saw my expression and quickened her pace. "Oh Em, how did you sleep?" She gave me a tight hug, folding my posture upright.

Initially, I didn't return her hug, scared that if I did I wouldn't be able to let go. In no time every limb of mine is grasped by my family – my feet, my hands, my head. My dad holds my shoulder. I can no longer not reciprocate. I squeeze my hands, wriggle my toes and return Mum's hug.

Dad's the first to break free from this family embrace. He pats my left shoulder and sits down in the green vinyl chair at the end of my bed. He crosses his arms, tight.

Kate perches on the end of my bed, she clasps her hands tightly around both my ankles. Mum holds my hands; her warmness engulfs my frozen limbs. In fact, she hasn't let go since entering the room, her handbag is still over her shoulder.

Bec gravitates from sitting to pacing to the door and back. Each time she gets up the plastic hospital sheets rustle. That and the tick of the clock and the distant buzzes of nurses' bells are the only sounds that enter the dread bubble we seem to all be in. It's almost like if we stay still and silent, we will delay time.

8.30 passes. Dad leaves to buy everyone coffees. Everyone but me. I am only allowed the little white tablets. I need something to fill my belly, there is too much room, the butterflies have become gigantic bats and are rapidly breeding and colliding.

By 9.30 Mum starts pacing the tiny room, "This is crazy," she says, looking out the door to her left and right like she is crossing a busy road.

"It's OK, Lyn; he'll come when he's ready," Dad says calmly from a visitor chair at the end of my bed. I wish Dad's calmness was contagious. We make small talk about the weather, the traffic, if the washing will dry, but the conversation is eventually exhausted. Eerie silence prevails.

"What's the time now?" I eventually ask, my voice shaky and high pitched with escalating fear.

Dad responds immediately, almost too quickly. He uncrosses his arms and glances at his silver wrist watch and gently puts his hand on my foot and says, "Close to 10am Em."

Out of everyone in the room Dad had looked quite relaxed. But his fast response proves that this seemingly calm posture is just a façade. I know he is being strong for all of us; that has always been his role in this family. But now his position is being tested. I nod and gulp, guilty for making him feel so awkward.

We all resume our positions in the room. Bec now moves up to sit near my torso and Kate and Mum's grip seems to only tighten. I need to go to the bathroom but I choose to hold on. I don't want to spend a second away from these people I love. *Separation anxiety is peaking.*

When the clock reads 10.30 I know that any minute I'll be taken away.

As if she's read my mind, the nurse enters, saying,

"Are you ready Dear? They'll be wheeling your bed in here shortly!" *No I'm not ready. I never will be.* I think to myself.

What do you say to the people you love when you may never see them again? I stumble over my words and end up saying, "So what are you guys going to do now?" I plug my tears, fixing my eyes on the pastel framed portrait on the far wall.

Bec lets goes of my finger, exchanging it for Mum's hand. I squeeze tightly onto a lifeless toy bear who's accompanying me to theatre.

"See you Ma," I blubber, turning my head to get a kiss on the cheek. A kiss that I'd once wiped off – embarrassed.

"You'll be fine, Em," Mum tries to reassure me, but her shaky soft voice is a dead giveaway that what happens now is totally out of her control.

At 10.35 a bubbly nurse enters suddenly with a clipboard.

"You all ready Emma?" she asks casually. I gulp the tears down and nod hesitantly.

A wheelie stretcher soon emerges, pushed by two males wearing scrubs and shower caps that match mine. They ask me a checklist of questions like, "Do you know what procedure you're having today?", "What part of your body are we operating on?" and "What's your birthdate?" They cross-reference with the details on my wrist band. Convinced this is me, they instruct me to lie down.

The cot sides slide upwards. The bed is turned and I'm wheeled away. I see my sisters huddled at Mum's side. My dad comes with me to hold my hand while they put me to sleep. I feel like a wuss but don't care.

Once inside the cold theatre all I see is faces in blue shower caps and facemasks. I smell disinfectant. Beeping sounds surround me. I taste tears, salty tears. I clench Dad's fist hard and the last thing I feel is a cold sharp sensation creeping up my arm.

Chapter 13
Things Don't Go According to Plan

My diary writing ceased there. The next part of my journey is put together with excerpts from my mum's diary, Dad's regular 'Emma Updates' and the recollections of my sister Bec and my friend Kiri.

Medical letter
Excerpt from Professor Michael Morgan's letter dated 27th June 2005 to Melbourne neurosurgeon Mr John McMahon

> Thank you for referring Miss Gee. As you know Emma was diagnosed with a right pontine arteriovenous malformation. She was admitted to Dalcross Hospital for definitive management of this lesion.
>
> On 17 June 2005, under general anaesthesia and with the aid of frameless stereotaxy, she underwent a retrosigmoid craniotomy, mastoidectomy and partial temporal free bone flap craniotomy. The transverse and sigmoid sinuses were able to be isolated and, immediately in front of the vein of Labbe, the

transverse sinus was ligated and divided with the dural opening both above and below the tentorium extending across to the free edge of the tentorium. This enabled further retraction forward of the sigmoid sinus, after the mastoidectomy, to facilitate an approach to the arteriovenous malformation. The AVM could be identified on the pial surface of the pons with clear evidence of surrounding haematoma. The arteriovenous malformation was resected on its margin and it was disappointing to see that the margin was not as well demarcated as many are in the brainstem. The AVM resection was complete and Emma went to Intensive Care.

Bec remembers ...

And then there was the waiting. Tick. Tick. Tick. Coffee. Tick. Tick. Tick. Banana bread. Tick. Tick. Tick. Talk to Mum or Kate about something. Tick. Tick. Tick. Sneeze. Tick. Tick. Tick. Look out the window. Yes, there was the waiting. Oh, and Dad's mobile phone. It sat in his hands like some crystal ball that was to throw some news, some future, some 'what would be' at us. It told us nothing so we went back to the hospital and played some more of the waiting game.

Mum's diary: 17th June 2005

At 4.30pm Professor Morgan came out to tell us all had gone well and that he thought the AVM was all removed. It was more difficult and deeper than he had thought. It's hard to believe you could work on something just 10mm in diameter for 7 hours – what an amazing, skilled man!

Bec remembers ...

All had gone well. She would wake up soon enough. Be OK. I blinked. Unblocked my ears. I needed to hear it again. Yes, she would be OK. Was it that easy? I wasn't prepared for this. It being so easy.

Kiri remembers ...

I'd stayed at a friend's house the night of Em's surgery, and I woke to the 'Message received' beep from my mobile. Wide awake at once, I grinned and breathed a sigh of relief to hear from Bec that Em was out of surgery – she was OK. I woke up my friend to tell her the good news, then slipped back into a weekend doze.

Mum's diary 17th June 2005

Em was slow to wake up so we decided to go back to my sister's place at Pymble for dinner ... We were all so relieved and happy to know the operation had gone well, but then suddenly Bec became terribly upset and said she had a dreadful feeling that things were not right for Emma. Five minutes later the phone rang. Professor Morgan, the surgeon. Em was not waking up and they were doing a CAT scan to ascertain why. Possibly she was bleeding!

Bec remembers ...

Dad turned white and told us that the professor had said there'd been a complication and Em was bleeding internally – that they had to go back in and operate again. I collapsed. Hollow. Gutted. Cried like I'd never cried. Dad left to sign some forms. I don't know where everyone else was. I know my aunt's lounge room was packed full of bodies. Aunts. Uncles. Cousins. I remember looking up and noticing how desperate it was. Nobody need say anything.

Our bodies sang desperation. A sea of distraught people. We were all connected. Hugging, linked, not wanting to let each other go. Em gone was enough.

Medical letter

Excerpt from Professor Morgan's letter dated 27th June 2005

> She was slow to wake up and appeared to have a left upper limb weakness so went for a CT scan immediately. This showed a haemorrhage extending from the bed of the AVM around the pons laterally toward the IVth ventricle. Because of the concern there may be residual AVM she was immediately returned to the operating room. There was no active bleeding but there were some small blood vessels that were difficult to distinguish between them being a small amount of residual AVM and enlarged feeding arteries, but this was likely to be the source of the haemorrhage. This was secured with micro clips and resected along with evacuation of some of the haematoma before she again was returned to the Intensive Care unit.

Mum's diary 17th June 2005

My brother Peter prayed with us as we sat around the lounge room stunned and waiting for news of the operation to stop the bleed found by the scan. The second operation was 9pm to 11pm, so we were so relieved when Prof Morgan rang to say that he had removed the remaining piece of AVM and sucked out the blood that had pooled in the cavity.

Kiri remembers…

It was a rude shock to receive a call a couple of hours later from the designated breaker-of-bad-news (Clare or Al? I can't remember ...) who was calling to say that Bec had, in her excitement, spoken too soon. Although Em's procedure had been completed, there had been some complications, a bleed, and she was now to remain in an induced coma to maximise her chances of recovery. My stomach dropped.

Mum's diary 18th June 2005

We went to see Emma in ICU – tubes coming out of her everywhere – so unbearable for any mum to see her child lying there so helpless and vulnerable. The stress is unbelievable but she is alive! A tense, tense night ahead.

Medical letter

Excerpt from Professor Morgan's letter to Mr John McMahon dated 27th June 2005

> Following this Emma is, not surprisingly, slow to wake up and she continues to have much of the findings she had prior to, and immediately after, the first surgery. Angiography at this time demonstrated complete resection of the arteriovenous malformation and I am hopeful her recovery will be continuous and productive.

Bec remembers …

From there on it's really a blur. One day was the same as the next. Wake up. Em awake? No. Try to eat. Go to hospital. Watch her, or somebody that lay in her bed that looked nothing like the Em I knew, try to breathe – live – breathe. Again, I was pretty good at not connecting. Being there without believing it was really how it would be. I had to believe she would be OK. I held her hand and told her to fight. Hang in there. I seriously imagined my energy channelling into her tiny frame, giving her a bit of a zap. God knows, I think at some point, on one of those days that felt like one long day, I even sang to her. No wonder she slept. I remember taking people in to see her. Uncles. Friends. Watching them cry. I had to be strong. Show them it would be OK.

I think the things I hated most were the machines. The beeping. Beep. Beep. Beeeeeeping. Was something wrong? Did I squeeze her hand too tight? Did I talk too loud? I hated the smell of it too. Hospitals have a musty medicated tang. A lingering air that just makes you feel trapped.

Dad's Emma update 18th June 2005 (the first of many emails to keep friends and family informed)
Our apologies for not letting you know what's been happening before now but, as you'll see, the last day or two has been fairly stressful for us all.

Em had her op for removal of an AVM yesterday. After a seven-hour procedure, all seemed to be well and the surgeon was pretty happy with the way things had gone. Unfortunately, last night she had a small bleed into the operation site and had to be taken back to theatre. Last night and today her condition has been stable but is still very serious. She will remain in intensive care for a few days. She is still asleep so we haven't been able to talk to her yet and needs assisted breathing so that the staff can properly control her functions whilst her brain heals. The next 72 hours will be critical. The good news is that today's angiogram showed that all of her AVM had been removed.

Thank you for your support, love and prayers. Please don't ring us at the hospital. Text messages and emails are great.

Mum's diary 19th June 2005

Another night Em has come through but still she's not awake partly because of her brain swelling and the bleed into the cerebellum and partly due to the sedation to stop her blood pressure getting too high ...We are all so tired with the tension and just hope we sleep tonight after lying there each night waiting for the phone to ring. Tomorrow is crunch day – 72 hours since surgery where the swelling maximises.

Dad's Emma update 20th June 2005

Thank you again for all your prayers, messages and emails. We feel very loved and supported. Em remains in intensive care. She is still critically ill, but the good news is she is stable and not deteriorating. Hopefully in the next day or two they will be able to wake her up. The medical and nursing staff here are fantastic and we have every confidence in them.

Mum's diary 21st June 2005

Tonight Dr Chia and Prof Morgan assured us that Em is progressing and that she had briefly opened her eyes, Prof Morgan said he was 95% sure she would wake up and that he's seen people come from a worse place to achieve full recovery. That was so reassuring and then Em not only squeezed our hand, but opened her eyes for us briefly. This was so exciting but frustrating that they have had to sedate her to keep her blood pressure low as the vessels in her brain heal better. Surely tomorrow will see more improvement!

I found out much later what had actually happened in my operation. The edges of the AVM were rather poorly defined. At the base of the AVM in my pons (part of the brain stem) it was difficult for the surgeon to distinguish between the abnormal vessels of the lesion and the normal vessels in the brain tissue that fed the AVM. So, by the end of the first operation, he thought he'd completely removed all of the abnormal tissue. He was worried that if he dug any deeper into the pons he would do more harm than good. Unfortunately for me, a few abnormal vessels were left behind and bleeding from these was responsible for the damage to the pons and the nerve tracts to the adjacent cerebellum (which controls balance). At the second operation the blood clot was removed and bleeding vessels were clipped off. The good news was the postoperative angiogram confirmed that all the AVM had now been removed.

But the bad news was I had had a haemorrhagic stroke. At that point it was unclear what that would mean.

Chapter 14
From Dreams to Reality

As my family sat around waiting and hoping that I would wake up, where was I? I was caught in a deep sleep, haunted by vivid dreams …

I'm standing in a spacious mezzanine-like room. The only thing in it is a large soft white bed almost floating on the carpeted platform. I'm standing on the spongy surface easily, both hands free. Steps lead down to a shiny white lino-surfaced corridor. It looks cold and hard. But I stay where I am. I'm content here. The sun beams through the panels of glass that enclose the room. I walk to the bed and, after kicking off my towelling slippers, I jump into it and snuggle with my teddy bear, warm under the covers. Brain surgery isn't so bad, I think, drifting off into oblivion.

I wake in a different room with no natural light. I'm lying on a cold, hard metal table and my body throbs. *Something isn't right.* Suddenly, noisy white-coated people surround me. I can only see their torsos. They seem distressed, their white arms move too quickly around me for my relaxed state. Their voices collide and I can't make out their words. I try and tell them to be quiet but I can't. I'm too tired.

I feel them move me. At the same time, a lightning bolt of pain strikes through me and my eyes are forced wide open. I try and jolt upright but my body seems restrained. A nurse slowly raises a thin metal pole vertically above my torso. She suddenly lowers it violently, piercing through the skin and puncturing my chest. Blood spurts onto the blue curtains around me. The red fluid leaks relentlessly from my stomach, gushing. Gushing so fast, too fast. I need to stop it. I move the teddy bear I'm clutching and try to mop up some of the fluid. The teddy's brown soft fur is now wet and dark red. Someone help me! I plead, but the white-coated people just stand around my bedside, arms crossed, watching me struggle and bleed. *Can't they see that I need help?* I lie there hollow, the pumping red fluid leaking out of me. I am helpless. Naked. Vulnerable. I am going to die.

A bright light enters the room and I seem to vanish, evaporate into the white starchy sheets. I soon emerge in a new, almost exotic landscape, fertile and moist. The harsh antiseptic stench is gone. Now gorillas replace the white-coated people. I feel strangely at home in this more natural landscape. The pain dissipates and I no longer feel exposed and vulnerable, even though I appear to be in an animal enclosure. Throughout my life I'd visited zoos and sanctuaries and as a child had been warned, "Don't go beyond the viewing areas." In my dream that childhood danger seems a myth. In this cage I feel so safe and accepted. My close family are let into the enclosure and given time to learn my language. I am excited to give them a tour. Others who step into my world are forced to adapt. There's a great feeling of relief being in a realm free of beeps and tubes and judgement, surrounded by gorillas.

I'm motionless but the world spins around me. Then suddenly it stops and, like being double-bounced when jumping on the trampoline, I go flying through the air, down, down, down. Falling. Out of control, I seem to go faster and faster and it gets colder and colder. Freezing. It becomes darker. Grey and black shades replace the warm colours of the gorilla world I've been taken from. I land with a thud on a cold surface, in a concrete box-like room. All of the walls are identical, no windows or doors. *Which way is up?* There are no voices, only the smell of moldy dampness, and it's bitterly cold. I'm terrified, but too tired to invest my energy in to fear. I curl into a ball on my side, and I sob. I feel completely alone and forgotten. The sound of my sobbing echoes off the walls even after the tears have been milked out of me. I am left here to die. *This must be hell!*

Later my auntie and uncle join me down in the coldness, adding a glimpse of warmth. Although colour is absent from the room, now shimmering light seems to bounce off my auntie's wrist. The glare hurts my eyes. At the same time, the beam of light keeps me awake and feels like it's preventing me from falling further into the coldness. *Are they saying goodbye? Why aren't my parents here?*

With a shock I realise that this cold room is actually a crematorium, a chamber for dead people. They think I am dead but I am still awake. I am alive. I just can't move to alert them. I'm trapped. Three astronaut-like suited people abruptly appear and move my corpse onto a metal stainless-steel bench on rollers, a bench that extends into a dark tunnel that leads to a hot furnace. Panic and terror engulf me. I have minutes before I will be burnt alive. *I'm still alive.* Frantic to escape this torment I try to move again, to signal that I am alive. I instruct my stubborn body to blink but my eyes won't close, they feel probed open. *How do I tell them that this 'corpse' is only masking the life trapped beneath?* This is not how I thought my life would end.

The three strangers stuff my body into the dark tunnel, like shoving overflowing toothpaste back into a narrow hole. My body is detached from my head. I am an observer of this torture. My head feels weighted, bulging. I peer inside my skull to see why. Clambering around and rudely invading my headspace are two people fighting. They're wearing matching lycra suits, the tiny female dressed in white and the male in black. As they leap and flip around the pain is excruciating. To me it is so clear that they don't fit, but they scramble around as if they had oodles of space. I watch from the sidelines. Their every move leaves a shocking bolt of pain. In their 'fight' intermission a mini nurse in white appears between them and holds up two outfits. One is black and plain, the fabric thick and rough. I run my index finger and thumb along the skirt's hem. It is lined, too, *surely too hot for a coffin?* The other dress is bright yellow with colourful dots scattered over the silky thin fabric like hundreds and thousands. "This one's perfect," I say. The nurse holds up the left hand of the white-lycra suited person and hands me the bright garment. The fight is over and the white girl has won. The black character is sprawled on the ground, defeated.

Suddenly, the grey concrete surface beneath me moves rapidly upwards. Up, up and up. Almost in fast-forward motion, cartoon-like. As the upward momentum stops, I fall back on a soft, warm surface and large hands pancake over my body, preventing any jerky motion. Calmness.

"You're OK, the operation went well," a voice says. I try to open my eyes.

~

Many people have asked me how I can still recall these dreams today. My reply is simple. They were so real and so traumatic. It's almost as if my brain was trying to make sense of the horrific operation.

Looking back on those dreams they seem full of metaphors. The warm white bed at the beginning was the comfort of sedation taking over. Maybe my brain was reassuring me that all would go as planned and I could just relax. When the scene abruptly changes and I find myself among the white-coated people, it is almost as if my brain is alerting me to the obscure and panic-filled danger ahead. Or was some part of me aware of what was happening in the operating theatre?

The swinging motion I experienced in the gorilla enclosure could have been my body adjusting to altered balance. Maybe the gorilla's incomprehensible language made my gibberish seem normal?

In those eight days of coma I was obviously aware of some things around me. I dreamt of my aunt and uncle and found out later they had been there saying prayers at my bedside and that my auntie was wearing a bright bracelet, which matched the bright light I saw coming from her wrist in the dream.

The fight between the black- and white-suited figures and the choice between the two garments do seem to symbolise some moment when there was a choice between life and death. The white figure winning and the selection of the yellow dress over the coarse coffin fabric perhaps meant that I chose life.

These coma dreams were like no other dreams I've ever experienced. They still haunt me day after day and still elicit nausea years later. I don't know if they'll ever fade.

In my attempt to banish these nightmares, months later I asked my therapists to jot down my recollections. In doing this I was attempting to differentiate them from reality. Even so, I couldn't decipher which realm I wanted to be in – they were both hell in their own way. The life I woke up to after those eight days of fantasies was in many ways harder to make sense of than my dreams.

Chapter 15
Waking Up

I'm awake internally but my body won't budge. I try to stir it again. *Move!* I command. I want to yawn and stretch out long and then turn onto my side in a warm foetal position. But I lie still. *How do I instruct this body?* It feels detached from my thoughts. It throbs, but I don't know where this awful sensation is coming from. In fact, I can't figure out where my body starts and ends. The pain seems to morph into the hard surface I'm lying on. It's an endless blur of agony.

"Wakey-wakey," a chirpy voice says loudly in my ear. I can feel a gush of warm air on my skin. What's frightening is that I *am* awake but my lazy body just won't shift! I feel like a kid again, hiding under my doona, but this time it's not my choice. My skin feels like it's thickening, suffocating me. Noises seem muffled and distant, as if I'm submerged under water.

Suddenly a bright light breaks through my impenetrable skin. The darkness turns into a glowing orange blur and my eyelids are probed open. "See if her pupils are dilated," a male voice commands, shining a pen torch in my direction. An unwanted beam of hot, stinging, yellow light enters my vulnerable body. *I'm not ready to be found yet.* The light beams from side to side, disco-like. My pupils are exposed like a deer in spotlights, vulnerable, immobilised and captured.

I gasp for breath. All I can see is a plastic dome blocking my blurry view, an oxygen mask. I had hoped to see a familiar face, or recognise a voice, but when I try to free myself, the clear plastic mask is held over my face. I can't move my arms to pull it off or squirm free.

A distinct flavour of stale blood coats the inside of my mouth. There's a disinfectant smell so strong I can taste it. These awful sensations are the only bridge for me from the terror lands of my dreams into what seems to be reality. *Where is this blood coming from?*

"Good afternoon, Emma," a deeper voice joins in my wake-up call. Then the voices exchange medical notes about my status. I want to join in their conversation. This discussion is about me after all. Shouldn't I be included? Has my operation gone OK? But their voices fade and once again I'm alone. I opt to sleep, to rest again to make sure I muster up enough energy to move or open my eyes for my next witness. The darkness has a heart beat.

Days pass and I drift in and out of this state, shifting from the internal terror of my dreams to awareness of an outside world I'm unable to communicate with. Neither of these places is where I want to be. I can't understand where my family is. I'm distressed and so confused by this. *I want my mum and dad!*

"Em, are you awake?" There's a voice to my right and someone is stroking my fingertips gently. I try to open my eyes, to let the light in. I don't want to be in this dark realm alone anymore. Through the slit in my eye I see blurred figures … fuzzy moving images. They spin around me, and a loud beeping blasts through my body. I want to tell them to stop moving and to turn the volume down. But my efforts exhaust me. I welcome the darkness and shut my eyes.

Bec remembers …

One day she woke. I want to say it was months after, years perhaps, but I think it was just over a week. How she was to begin with scared me a lot. She made funny noises, couldn't swallow, her eyes rolled different ways. Somebody I could understand completely for as long as I remembered was underneath it all – I knew that – but at that point I felt like I'd be forever digging to find her.

When I muster the effort to keep my eyes open, what I see is not what I expect. The room is tilted, like a boat, and spinning like a fast ride I'd once been on at the Melbourne show. Images are double. Two of everything. Cloned machines and two tubes sprout from my arm. *I have been a twin for 24 years; maybe it's my turn to see two?* Like a disjointed slide show, the blurry images gravitate around each other. The world is moving but I am still. Tubes grow from my body like roots from a tree. The bags of fluid connected to these tubes are the only moving things. I can feel the invasive cold fluid travel around my blood stream. I taste blood. I smell fear. Everything to do with this body is now foreign.

Mum's diary June 24th 2005

We went down to see Em at 11am as usual and were so excited to hear that she was awake and they were removing the tube that was draining fluid from her head. She squeezed our hands and tried to open her eyes and to talk – a huge improvement on yesterday! The staff were so excited, and I tried to be, but seeing her half awake and so frustrated as she tried to tell us things was so difficult. I have to balance that with being grateful that she is alive and improving.

The subsequent days pass slowly, too slowly. Actually, I don't know if it is days or weeks. My new routine involves being cleaned, rolled and fed by a stranger in darkness. Poked. Prodded. Pinched. Occasionally I see the familiar face of a family member, but their short visits only seem to highlight the distress I'm in. I try to speak to them behind the mask, but what comes out is just muffled and only seems to elicit frowns. *How can they expect me to speak clearly with a plastic thing over my mouth? Take it off! Why are the lights off? Why are they whispering?* They leave before I can murmur back to them. I need to tell them what's going on so they can get me out – make them see that I need to escape this hell I'm trapped in.

Noise is torture. The constant humming of the fluorescent lights is soon joined by the collision of rubber soles with the lino floor. Each footstep causes a high-pitched scream inside my head. *Why do I have no idea which direction these sounds are coming from?* I can't anticipate their direction because my eyes won't budge sideways and my neck won't turn. The nurse has positioned my head in a downward direction and all I can see is lots of feet below the curtain at the end of my bed. The ripping sound of the curtain, as the thin, blue material is gathered along the silver track above my bed, penetrates my entire body and reverberates painfully in my head.

Every hour, the curtains are drawn, two staff enter and then, "on the count of three" I am turned. I feel like a tangled chain of kabana at the butcher. Although I'm just being rolled over in standard hospital style, to me it feels like I'm continually being spun around and around and around in a hammock. "Enough!" I inwardly shriek. "This is too much. *This is not fun.*" As a kid on a swing I'd loved this kind of adrenalin rush, the grey metal chains twisting and spinning me. Now it is terrifying and I feel permanently out of control. After each turn, the dizzy blur doesn't ease, and the double images spin around me in constant motion. I close my eyes but my world keeps spinning.

Mum's diary 25th June 2005

Em looked so sick today. Her eyes were wandery and her mouth and tongue were worrying her. She just didn't look like Em! Dr Chia is pleased with her, though, and says the speaking will come. When I asked about that he said, 'We need to remember she has had a major operation. Only a handful of surgeons in the world would've operated on this AVM and it was deeper and more complex than they thought'. In fact, he said she is very lucky to be alive! Although she has a facial palsy, he says it's only partial and will probably go with time … Kate just burst into tears and we all felt so depressed and sad for Em, despite Dr Chia's assurance. It just breaks your heart to see her so lost and sad and helpless. If only she could speak to us and tell us how it is for her but maybe she's not remembering too much of this. Hopefully not.

White-coated figures surround my bed, one with crossed arms, the others holding pens and clipboards. Black stethoscopes coil around their necks. *Do they ever use these or are they just to show their status?*

"What day is it Emma?" a deep voice asks.

In this darkness I can't even differentiate night from day. I have no idea. I try to say that but they don't understand me. "It's Tuesday today, Emma, and it's a cold morning outside," he explains, in a slow monotonous tone. There are no windows to glance out to prove he's telling the truth about the weather. *Why don't they show me? Take me outside, give me some fresh air and let me see for myself.* At the same time he moves to take my pulse, to find the bloodstream that's apparently keeping me alive. His fingertips tap my wrist firmly; his nails begin to pinch my skin. *Ouch! How do I tell him that it hurts?*

The questions posed now become commands. "Now can you squeeze my hand, Em?"

"Blink."

"Wriggle your toes."

I do as they say but there's a delay in my ability to perform these actions. They leave my bedside before I have a chance to show them that I understand. They're giving up already.

Mum's diary 27th June 2005

Today Em was up in a chair when we arrived. This was good as her chest mustn't be congested and she's been lying down for so long. Still she is unable to talk, poor kid. Having double vision as well is just awful and yet they are really happy with her progress. We only stayed a short time because she was so tired. Her right eyelid doesn't close properly so it's hard to tell when she's asleep and I hope they might tape that tonight.

I'm still in intensive care.

"Now Emma, the doc says that to get out of here we have to get you drinking, get your fluids up." A nurse sits next to me balancing a tray on her lap with a spoon, a plastic jug and a cup. She drops two spoonfuls of a thick, white substance from a large jug into a plastic mauve cup. I choke unless all fluids are thickened. With a teaspoon, she brings it to my mouth. I'm confused. *I'm meant to drink to get out of this prison, but this isn't fluid.*

"Open your mouth, Sweetie," she instructs and opens her own mouth wide hoping that I'll copy her. The teaspoon is pressed against my lips, waiting for permission. I tell my brain to widen my mouth but it refuses to cooperate.

"Open wide," she repeats impatiently.

I feel like a toddler refusing to eat. She forces the teaspoon between my lips and scrapes the tasteless metallic clag-like contents against my teeth. It pools in my mouth and then seeps out, the clear muck dangles. The nurse wipes me, saying, "Let's clean you up, Sweetie, it's all over your chinny chin chin." *Great, I'm drooling and I can't even tell. I can't swallow this stuff. Perhaps if she tasted it she'd know why.*

Dad's emma update 25th june 2005

We've had a few roller-coaster days with Em's level of awareness increasing to the point that they could remove her endotracheal tube. This was great news, as was the news this morning that her brain scan did not reveal any new problems. However, whereas she was so "peaceful" when asleep she is now a little restless and confused as the effects of her brain swelling and the prolonged sedation are more apparent. It will take a few days before she is really "awake" and can talk to us. She does know that we are there but you sense that she is struggling to respond to our questions about how she is feeling. This is all distressing for us, especially Bec who, of course, can sense what her twin feels.

Mum's diary 28th June 2005

We came back this afternoon but didn't stay long. Em either gets too stressed trying to tell us things or too tired and we can only go in two at a time anyway.

Each visit from my close family brought warmth and familiarity into the stark environment. But I couldn't understand why I only ever saw one or two of them at once and why they only stayed for a short time. *Have they given up on me? Do they have something better to do? Why do they look so glum?*

Their complexions were greyish, the worry zapping any colour. They seemed upset. If only I could move to comfort them, I thought. But it was they who were trying to cheer *me* up. My sisters paint my toenails bright pink. The colour is a welcome contrast to the cold whites and greys of my surroundings. I know, though, that I will need something way brighter than nail polish to fully wake up this body and help me on my road to recovery.

Chapter 16
Reality Bites

As the medication was reduced and I became more alert, I started to get an inkling of what had happened to me. All the time in ICU I'd convinced myself it was the drugs that had been stopping me from getting back to being my old self. *How could I recover with all the hospital paraphernalia, the mask and tubes smothering me?* Now it slowly dawned on me that even my close family couldn't understand me. I longed to communicate and escape the terror I was trapped in. But I couldn't, the words inside me seemed set in concrete.

They call on Bec, hoping that as my identical twin she may comprehend my gibberish. But she just shakes her head at my attempts to communicate. Her lips begin to tremble and eyes well up with tears. She has no idea. My family attempts a few different things to try to communicate with me. At one point my sister holds a pen in my right hand, angle my head at the paper and say, "OK now write how you feel, Em."

Easy, I think. But again, the letters are stuck inside my head. If only I could write, *I am terrified.* Instead I become so distressed my blood pressure rises with my heightening frustration. In seconds the nurse is with us and is simultaneously grabbing the paper and pen from her and sternly saying, "You'll have to stop that and go." Without giving me a chance to compose and transcribe how I feel, she whisks Bec away. I am alone with my stuck words and boiling frustration.

Determined, Bec arrives a few days later with a red magnetic letter board under her arm and a big grin as if to say, "I don't know why I didn't think of this earlier." I inwardly smile back – *finally a way to communicate!* She holds the board near my right hand and puts the loose letters in my flaccid fist, wrapping her fingers around my useless digits to guide them. But she must've lathered the colourful letters in soap as they're too slippery to grip. *This is not a time to play tricks, Bec*, I silently huff. My blood pressure goes up again.

Student doctors surround my bed and assume their examination stances. *This is my chance to prove that I am still cognitively OK.* It is a test of my cranial nerves, something I struggled with when I studied anatomy. No time for last-minute cramming or Red Bull fixes to kick-start my brain. I have waited all morning for this. Since their last visit I'd practised moving my head in a nodding action, my chin falling quickly to my chest with no control. It's a way of communicating a definite 'Yes.'

I think, "I'll show them this."

I try to block out the constant high-pitched buzzing in my head. I listen hard to their commands and do my best to obey, desperately attempting to shrug my shoulders, to squeeze both eyes shut, to purse my lips. But my body refuses to do what my brain tells it to. I can't even raise an apologetic smile. They don't seem too impressed at my efforts. I watch them jot notes on their clipboards in silence. They soon leave. Deflated and utterly exhausted, I sleep.

I opted to have this procedure. I chose to have my head cut open to remove the teeny weeny thing in my brain. Although I'd heard the associated risks and signed my will, deep down I thought the chance of anything bad occurring was unlikely. In my mind I had thought I would get this over and done with and return to my life as a normal 24-year-old, living independently, running and working full-time again. Becoming disabled was not part of this plan. My wonderful family seemed optimistic that I would soon make a full recovery. But I was starting to suspect that it wasn't going to be quite that simple.

Chapter 17
Deficits Revealed

Mum's diary 30th June 2005

We were so pleased to find Em out of ICU – in Room 10 downstairs near the nurses' station.

Apparently I had 'eaten' enough fluid and was choking less, so could be transferred to my own room on the ward. It was a relief to move from ICU, but at the same time it concerned me that the doctors thought I was well enough to not need constant medical supervision. *Surely I wasn't safe to be alone yet? I still hadn't been allowed to get up!* The constant presence of medical staff had become familiar and was comforting.

The room I was moved to was even brighter and noisier next to the nurses' station. While that made me feel secure, my brain couldn't cope with all the extra stimulation. My new body interpreted every noise or touch as severe pain. Any slight movement elicited waves of nausea. It was far from the stillness I'd envisaged. This new place only seemed to cause more discomfort. The walls still spun anticlockwise, and the lights seemed brighter. I still saw double, and the cloned strangers wouldn't let me sleep. They made my tired body sit upright but didn't seem to understand that they'd tipped the chair on a 35-degree angle. It was impossible to sit without falling forward.

The truth was dawning. I had had a stroke. *I'm too young to have had a stroke. I'm an active healthy girl. Aside from the odd cold, I've never been to many doctors. Plus, I'm an OT. This shouldn't happen to me. My patients have strokes, not me!* But there was no doubt. I'd had a bleed in my brain and acquired all these deficits. My medical file now had a long recent history. Dysphagia, dysarthria, nystagmus, diplopia, sensory, balance and mobility deficits. All big medical terms that I thought I understood in theory but was now experiencing first hand. Terms that I used daily as a health professional, and seemed to stress the importance of my role and add to my credibility. Now I was beginning to see that, to a patient, they were just gobbledygook, adding unnecessary confusion and complexity to their situation. How differently I viewed the medical jargon now that it applied to my own body.

In plain English, I had trouble swallowing and needed tubes shoved inside my throat to help me (*dysphagia*); people couldn't understand me (*dysarthria*); I wobbled like jelly (*ataxia*); I couldn't point directly at anything and approached any object in a zig-zag fashion (*dystonia*); my world was angled (*vertigo*); I couldn't control my bowels and needed a catheter to wee (*double incontinence*); I now saw two of every image – and trust me, seeing one bed pan was enough! – (*diplopia*); my world now spun (*nystagmus*). My left hand clawed in like a scared turtle hiding in its shell (*left-side paralysis*); my mouth permanently drooped to the right, my eye wouldn't close and I drooled (*right-side facial paralysis.*) But wait, there was more. They were predicting that my balance and mobility would also be an issue when I got out of bed as the bleed was in my cerebellum, the control centre for balance.

I dreaded how many more deficits I had yet to discover. At just 24 I had been in full flight. Now, my wings had been clipped. I may no longer fly.

Mum's diary 30th June 2015

Prof Morgan came in and told us she "had all her marbles". It is so good to know she doesn't have permanent brain damage even if her speech, facial nerves and left side are temporarily affected.

Although I was barely verbal and attempted badly to use a communication board, my surgeon had assessed my cognitive state in other ways, and it was an immense relief to hear him say that I still had 'all my marbles'. Every word I had tried to say or spell in those initial weeks had been communicated with one intention – to show everyone that I was still mentally OK. I also assumed that the wooziness, inability to move, speak or swallow would resolve … not worsen. But as days passed my newly acquired deficits became more and more apparent.

Previously I'd felt like I was only a head, as my body had felt too heavy and numb to own. Now it had woken up and joined my head. But it felt as though the surgeons had incorrectly welded the two body parts together. Like a marriage gone wrong, they clashed from the beginning of my journey and refused to co-operate.

Each day, the reality of my damaged body sank in more. I would finally begin to get used to one deficit just to find I had another to deal with. On about day 17 a really odd sensation emerged. I started to feel water streaming down my right cheek, and kept a tissue in my useable right hand to try to mop up the imaginary fluid. Puzzled, my visitors noticed my new weird habit and tried to assure me that I was not leaking.

I also experienced other phantom symptoms in those early days. The beginnings of my chronic nerve pain emerged, my damaged brain sending strange signals to my body. My pain seemed trapped inside my tight skin. Any movement, particularly in my left arm, automatically shook up the fiery thick balls of pain. They angrily rammed into each other as they tried to penetrate the skin to escape. If I lay still, the pain seemed to settle and, although still constant, appeared to simmer away deep down. "Don't move," I pleaded.

While I hated understanding so much of the medical jargon, having worked in the health sector meant I could draw on some of my experiences dealing with other patients. As an OT I'd worked in pain management and I thought I knew how debilitating chronic pain could be, but this was different. It was a storm, unbearable, nothing like I'd ever experienced. I was determined to start desensitising my own warped, wrongly wired body as soon as possible. I would test if the pain management strategies I had prescribed for others actually worked.

Despite the pain, I knew I had to force my body to move. One method I used in those early days was just moving my fingers – tapping each finger pad to thumb one by one. I'd repeat the pinching action with each digit simultaneously with my right and left hand. While my right side seemed to struggle with the movement, it was the pain and hypersensitivity in my left hand that slowed it down and enabled my right to keep up.

Another deficit that revealed itself was ataxia. Every time I went to move or reach for something my body shook rigidly in an exaggerated shiver. This horizontal shudder confused anyone watching. They were unable to work out what I wanted. My body felt like it had become possessed.

The first time I walked I needed a physio and two nurses to support me. Each strongly gripped a limb or section of my uncooperative puppet-like body. I was so bendy that they all struggled to coordinate my limbs. Apparently, in that initial attempt I only walked three metres. A few months before, three kilometres had been a tiny distance. Unable to walk me, they returned me to a huge bear-like chair that was so soft it almost swallowed me. Exhausted, I slept.

When I wake I see a young girl staring directly at me. "Look at her," I gasp inwardly. "Poor thing." Her weak, pale body occupies a similar chair to mine. Her body seems flaccid, her limbs strapped in. Her torso is tilted to one side, angled like she's about to fall asleep. A white folded pillow acts as a bumper, positioned on her right shoulder, and forces her neck to sit upright. Her facial features look wrong, asymmetrical, almost like a mosaic we'd studied in art at school. She only has one eye – the other is hidden behind a white eye pad, and her mouth is askew. She's obviously had surgery on her head. The right side is shaven and staples bridge a 20cm bloody incision. Greasy tufts of hair sprout from the other side of her skull … Then the blue knitted poncho around her neck catches my eye. *That's the garment my grandma gave me! Why is she wearing it too*? With a shock I realise it's mine and this is *my* reflection. *This is … me. This is* me. *What has happened to me? This girl is me.* Terror surrounds and engulfs me.

Chapter 18
At the Mercy of Staff

The nurse enters, her vicious bright red mouth sighs loudly before she crouches down out of my sight at the end of my bed. *Where has she gone?* A waft of urine wacks me before I can hold my breath – she's emptying my catheter or 'handbag' that accompanies me to my twice-daily physiotherapy sessions. "You must drink more fluid if you want us to take this out, Dear," she warns, holding up the full catheter bag at a great height. Without waiting for a response, she swivels on her heels and exits my room saying, "Just taking a break for a ciggy."

As I became more awake and aware of my surroundings I found my life depended on and was dominated by hospital staff. In my former life nurses and other health professionals were just part of the team, but now as a patient my relationship with them was quite different. I was helpless, a child, so reliant on their good grace to get through each day. And, as in all cases, there were wonderful staff members and those who were not so kind. Some, without realising it, made me feel quite humiliated in my new role.

In those first weeks I was unable to look after my most basic personal needs, like washing my hair. The long blonde strands

I had left on one side were greasy and streaked with dried red blood. The nurses would tie this remaining hair on the top of my head like a fountain. I couldn't wash it till the Frankenstein staples in the other side of my head were removed.

~

"OK, let's get these staples out," says the nurse, after parting my remaining hair as if looking for nits.

Was she sure? These metal clips clamped my head together and, although I hated them, I could wait. Besides I've already endured ten days of not washing what's left of my hair. But she is ready, even if I'm not. She slips on a pair of rubber gloves, grabs a green kidney dish full of instruments and fiercely clamps a pair of giant tweezers.

"Now just sit still and let me get these buggers out," she instructs, through clenched teeth. *Sit still? Even if I wanted to squirm free, I couldn't!* I try to close my eyes.

"Gawd I've had an awful morning today. I woke with a horrendous headache and haven't felt right all morning – think I need another coffee," she says, plucking the metal clips from my skull. *Am I hearing right? She's complaining of a coffee-deprived headache while plucking these things one by one from my head. Plus she is carrying out this procedure when she's tired. Great!*

~

Although I was feeling so traumatised being in this new body, I felt forced by the hospital environment to keep up. For me each event I faced was enough to deal with in a lifetime, but to others it was just part of the daily hospital checklist of tasks. I didn't have time to recover from one activity before being thrown into the next. The staff seemed to think that if I was given time to contemplate the difficulty of what was happening, I would never move forward. So in just one day I had a shower, a physio session, a 'feed' and the staples removed from my head. Visitors were yet to swarm.

To help me swallow, the speech therapist taught my feeders to stroke my neck to encourage the food 'downwards'. Although having someone's finger running down your neck isn't that pleasant, it did reduce the pooling of the awful tasting blobs of mush in my mouth. They had warned me before the op that my taste buds could be damaged. But when I first tried pureed cabbage I knew that they were OK. *Who purees cabbage?* It was just as disgusting as I expected it to be. At least the stroking strategy seemed to minimise the coughing fits and spluttering from choking on the mush. But not all strategies used by my carers were helpful. One nurse thought it would be a novelty to play the 'aeroplane game' with my food. Trying to track the flying puree was demeaning. I longed to return to eating normal, solid food again.

Often being young, mute and mentally alert made me the perfect sounding board for nurses' concerns. I'd lie there unable to sleep while their caffeine-loaded bodies dumped their personal sagas into my vulnerable ears. One nurse interpreted my night 'buzzing' for a drink as boredom. She danced my toy lion around my bed, putting on a deep voice. "My name's Simba the lion, I will protect you." She seemed to think she was entertaining a kid. I lay there thirsty and humiliated.

I longed for a means to convey my needs. The images on the communication board given to me by my speech therapist were so tiny I had difficulty seeing them. Also, my ataxia meant that my shaky indecisive fingers would inevitably point to the wrong picture. I'd be bombarded with piles of white hospital blankets when the truth was I was hungry! Eager to lessen my frustration and understand my needs, Bec drew a picture board with large icons. A later version was a letter board, a keyboard printed on paper. I managed to shakily spell out 'CAT' and 'MUM' but in my mind I needed to spell out something to prove to my therapist that I was all there. I decided on the words ENERGY CONSERVATION. With hindsight I don't know what medication I was on, but it was a health term that I thought would connect us as health professionals. It might prove to her that I still had a sense of humour.

The speech therapist enters and my sister Kate, also an OT, sits on the side of my bed. "Afternoon, Emma. How's your board going?" she asks.

On cue, I start spelling out my chosen words. As I hover over a letter, Kate says it out loud for me, pre-empting the possible word to save me unnecessary pointing. "It's 'E' for 'EMMA' and 'N' for 'Nellie', it's umm 'ENER" for ahhhh 'ENERGY'!" I try to smile. *She's saved me two letters.*

Then I continue and Kate looks confused, "There's more, Em?"

I nod. I can't afford to stop. I'm tired but determined. C. O. N. and so on … I get to V and I'm so exhausted I give up.

Suddenly Kate perks up and proudly says, "Conservation … it's Energy Conservation!"

We look at each other in relief. At last, a breakthrough in our communication. I had finally proved that beneath all this physical impairment, I was still here. Kate chuckles at my attempt to show a bit of humour. But the therapist doesn't seem to share Kate's enthusiasm. The 30-minute session is over, and I'm exhausted. Ironically in spelling out that word, I had done the opposite to what I'd intended – all my energy had been exhausted rather than conserved.

I close my eyes and sleep until dinner. I'll prepare for a three-word phrase next, but now I'll rest.

After the stitches were taken out came another milestone – the day they removed the catheter. *What a relief!* But then my continence was tested. If I sensed I needed to do a wee I'd call the nurses and they would assist me to the toilet. Often I'd try so hard but there'd be no action, even when they tried the running water technique. One nurse saw my inability to go as a huge time waster and, with a long, loud huff and a look at her watch, stood about one metre from me, expecting me to go. How could I when she was hovering over me? I was toilet training again.

My greatest toilet humiliation, though, was with using my bowels. I hadn't had a bowel action since waking from my coma. Those advertisements on tellie, marketing laxatives like Nulax, saying that being constipated made you feel "sluggish and irregular" were true. I felt gross, my bloated belly unable to store any more puree. Action was taken. I don't know what they put in my mushy food, but the result was dramatic…

I wake lying in a wet mound of my own faeces. The Coloxyl has worked. I buzzed for help, but am left in this volcanic eruption of my own bodily fluids for what seems like hours. My belly gurgles violently, like the sound of an InSinkErator eating hungrily the remaining kitchen waste. The nurse had shovelled the bitter white substance into my mouth assuring me that it would help "my tummy begin to work more normally". This explosion has not restored normality.

Finally footsteps come my way and my light goes on. "Oh gosh," the nurse gasps. She shouts loudly, "The Coloxyl has definitely worked in Bed 21! Can someone help me?" Her voice is now muffled through clenched teeth. "BYO gloves!"

Mortified, I close my left eye and let one tear roll down my left cheek. Soon enough I hear more people around me. Serious voices, a giggle (perhaps this is in my head), the sound of rubber gloves, and the clunk of my bed's cot sides collapsing. Then I'm rolled onto my side, so my bed-clothes and linen can be changed and my entire posterior-side wiped. Then one deep voice instructs, "We'll roll her on three. Nancy – you pull down her pants, Sylvia get the sheets ready and Bianca you wash her down. I'll roll her." I hear the shuffles, running water and the flap of sheets as they assume their positions.

Then I feel someone firmly grip my right shoulder, the other grabs my right hip, "Ready one … two … and three," she barks.

I groan, disliking the rocking movement. I feel like I'm on the Gravitron at the Melbourne show. My world spins fast. I feel giddy, nauseous, but I have nothing left for this body to expel. My throat gurgles but I know it's just crying wolf, like all the warning bells my body has set off since my operation. I'm angled sideways until my nose is squashed between the hard plastic mattress protector and the nurse's dimpled leg. Her chubby elbows then flex, tilting me on an angle to give them better access to the faeces aftermath. The nurse nods, instructing them to wipe me. "I'll get rid of this soiled stuff and get it ready for Mum to take home and wash."

I hear her tie a bag and drop the heavy parcel inside my cupboard ready for Mum to take when she next visits. Her words leave me filled with dread. Mum has enough to deal with. *She did this for me 23 years ago.* If I could yell, "My mum's name is Lyn and please chuck them in the bin," I would. If only my stupid body would work for ten seconds I would run and dispose of any evidence of this nightmare. *Yep, I would run to prevent my mum willingly sharing the humiliation I feel.* Being vulnerable and exposed is awful enough. Showing someone who already knows the last safe bits you're holding onto inside, when they know how it'll affect you, is hell. I gasp as a potent lemon disinfectant odour wafts over me. This, combined with the sickly sweet fake lavender deodoriser they spray, hovers in the air around me, so strong I am forced to taste it.

"All done, Emma." She squeezes my shoulder sympathetically and says, "You must feel quite embarrassed, but it's our job, Em. We do it all the time. Sleep now." Her voice is soft but tired, and my light is turned off.

~

Some nurses made me feel like a person rather than a patient. Jacqui was my favourite. She would carry out each task cheerfully without complaint. Even when giving me a sponge bath, rather than leave me lying naked on the bed, she would only uncover the necessary parts, ensuring that I remained warm and maintained the tiny bit of dignity I still had. She made me feel special, whether opening my curtains for some sunshine, or reading my get-well cards. She listened to my muffled speech and grunts and patiently attempted to figure out what I was saying, and moisturised my dry feet.

At night Lee and Ruby continued the amazing care that Jacqui had shown. Lee was so gentle in her manner and wore her soft grey hair in a bun on the top of her head, reminding me of a fairy-tale godmother. In her presence I slept better, knowing I was in good hands.

Actually, most of the night nurses were amazing. Knowing they were awake and watching me was so reassuring. I never would've endured that initial phase of my recovery without the generous care I received. My writings capture very humiliating and demeaning situations that prevailed in my diary and mind. I tell these stories to highlight the enormous impact another's words or actions can have on one's recovery. Being aware of those tiny things, often overlooked, can make all the difference.

Chapter 19
Passing on the Worry Baton

Being in Sydney meant the majority of my friends and work colleagues could not visit. Many of my relatives lived nearby and were so accommodating and supportive of my immediate family who'd travelled from Melbourne to be with me. I quickly realised just how big and how close my family was. Aunts. Uncles. Cousins. Great Aunts. More cousins. I loved seeing all this family. Each visitor left me with gifts and flowers. My Auntie Liz even smuggled her new dog into the 'pet-free' hospital in her carpet bag to cheer me up. But having so many people around also zapped my little energy.

Although I was distressed that those who knew me well could not understand me, having more than one person in the room was so comforting. My sister-in-law Rach would sing to me, and my siblings held my foreign limbs warmly. None of us had words to express the situation we were in. I'm sure they each put on a brave face for every visit and I can't begin to fathom how hard it was to see me in that state. For me it was somewhat easier, as I had medication to cloud the reality of the new realm I was in.

A regular visit from my parents was the major comfort in my new world. Where each visit was groundhog day and probably boring and tiresome for them, it was a highlight for me and gave me a reason to improve. A typical visit went something like this...

"Morning Em." Mum cheerfully disguised the sadness she must have been feeling. Seeing your daughter wrapped up in blood-stained bandages is not something any mother wants to see. Her tears bubbled in the background and, like a boy's pubescent voice, her pitch throughout the visits fluctuated. I knew that when she left the room to fill up jam jars for my flowers, she was probably filling them with tears. I couldn't move to comfort her. I couldn't turn to look away. I was forced to watch her fragile bravery.

She leant down and kissed me. I was unable to tell her that her body weight on the mattress worsened my pain. My bed's cot sides were positioned up to prevent me falling out, meaning she couldn't sit on my bed. Instead, she pulled over a chair and leant towards me. "It's quite cloudy out there today, Em. I think it'll rain again. But that's great for the garden ..." When she was there I could rest. Exhausted, I selfishly passed the worry baton onto her and slept.

I woke to a piercing *click click click* noise. Mum was knitting a blue beanie for my niece or nephew. She'd already knitted the white and pink ones. *I wish she could knit me a new body*. Every visit she brought crosswords, read get-well cards and I pretended to take in what she was saying, but the rhythmical tone of my mum's voice was soothing enough.

When Dad came he always chose to sit in my new black wheelchair. I liked that. He brought familiarity to the ugly device. His choice to sit in it instead of in the vacant visitor chairs was comforting. To me, without saying anything, he was accepting that his daughter now used a wheelchair. Sitting back in it, he appeared quite relaxed. Every day he helped me do my speech exercises. We poked out our tongues, did "eee" sounds, blew kisses and I tried to smile. The black footplates, adjusted for my two weak, flaccid legs, were his footrests. His twitching feet, which had always irritated me, were a rhythm of relief, a comforting metronome-like beat.

Apparently while I was in a coma my dad had said, "Em, when you wake up we'll buy you that golden retriever." Although I didn't recollect this promise, Bec was present. Determined to make him keep his word, she immediately began researching golden retriever litters. Talking about my future puppy became a diversion for my visitors and me in that initial stage. It was nice to hear people around me talking about things unrelated to my condition and seeing them smile for a change. But deep inside I began to silently freak out. *I had to care for a puppy and couldn't even toilet, wash or feed myself*. I couldn't communicate my reservations and my walls soon became plastered with photographs of the litter. The dog was chosen and the breeder agreed to keep him until I was back in Melbourne and able to care for him. Although I had always intended to name my first dog 'Gilbert', my family named him 'Morgan' after my surgeon, who I don't think was too impressed. He said, "I've had a baby named after me but … never an animal."

My parents didn't seem angry about their daughter's transformation. They were continually saying, "It'll be OK, Em, we're praying for you. It'll just take time." Whilst their words were reassuring, it was my body that had been tampered with. *Couldn't they just return it, like a faulty toy? Why did they seem so accepting? Why didn't they tantrum on my behalf?*

Towards the end of my stay at Dalcross Hospital many of my closest friends flew up from Melbourne. I knew it must have been so confronting to see me in the state I was in. But it was so reassuring to know they were there. They would take turns feeding me and wiping the drool off my face. I'm sure they would exit and burst into tears. *How was this fair? In a few short weeks I'd reverted to babyhood – soft toys, mashed food and afternoon naps.*

Bec had taken a lot of time off work, so once I was out of ICU she had to return to Melbourne and pick up her life. I hated her leaving, moving forward when I was going backwards. I was now in the negatives. Unable to freeze time while I caught up, Bec left me with Mum and Dad. My mind was filled with irrational distress. *Was this my pay back for entering the world seven minutes before her?*

Although inwardly annoyed at everyone's seemingly easy transition back into their 'normal' lives, on the outside I tried hard to not let this selfish mindset affect them.

Emma update 9th July 2005

Emma continues to improve slowly but it will be a long while before she is back to her old cheerful self. Although her legs are OK, her balance is poor and she can't yet stand without assistance.

Medical letter

Dr Alan Lam's letter to Professor Michael Morgan, dated 11th July 2005

> Having assessed Ms. Gee, I agree that she will require inpatient neuro-rehabilitation to optimize her transfers, mobility, function, swallowing, articulation, balance

> and co-ordination. She is currently not yet able to take a commercial flight back to Victoria with her parents. With the agreement of Ms. Gee and her parents, she will commence inpatient neuro-rehabilitation in Dalcross Private Hospital . Her program will entail Physiotherapy, Occupational Therapy and Speech Therapy.
>
> On successive reviews by me on the 7.7.5 and 9.7.5, Ms. Gee was making excellent progress. Her febrile illness was settling with antibiotics. The nasogastric tube has been removed because she is eating well and meeting her nutritional requirement, and her sitting balance and tolerance are improving. As such, Dr. Robert Chia, Intensivist, and I are hoping that she will be well enough to travel back to Victoria with her parents by commercial flight in about a week, so that she may continue inpatient neuro-rehabilitation in a public rehabilitation centre close to her home.

My departure from Dalcross was imminent. My close family and friends, who had already invested so much in my recovery, definitely deserved some acknowledgement for the tiny progress I'd made. Having worked in neuro I knew that it was going to be a very slow recovery. My journey had only just begun, and I would still need them for a long time yet. *How could I even begin to repay them for their efforts?* They knew that I still had my marbles but I wanted to somehow show them that their support had been worthwhile.

I still remember my mum's mobile number. I buzz the nurse and ask for the phone to be moved to my tray in front of me.

Instead of lifting the receiver, I lie there rehearsing pressing the blue padded digits on the phone in my mind. *I only have one chance to do this before my little energy vanishes*. But little do I realise how difficult it is to move and isolate my disobedient and ataxic fingers.

After a few hopeless attempts at punching the numbers in the right order and intermittent power naps, I somehow do it. I don't know what gibberish I mutter, but the weight of the phone kills me. So after Mum knows that it is me I drop the receiver. I'm so relieved that I've done it, but at the same time I'm frustrated. *What I'd rehearsed to say in my head had not come out*. I also had not prepared myself for the immense physical effort it would place on my weak body. Neither had I factored in the mental toll it would take trying to get my trapped words into action.

Mum's diary: 12th July 2005

While I was shopping my phone rang and a little voice said, "Ma … !" I couldn't believe it, but Em had rung me by herself. I'm amazed that Em, with her ataxia and eye problems, could dial by herself. What an achievement!

If I could dial a phone number, I surely could return to doing other normal things, and was determined to put in the effort.

Chapter 20
Handballed to Talbot

After weeks of preparation, I finally left Dalcross Hospital in NSW via ambulance with my mum. Dad met us at Melbourne airport and took us directly to Royal Talbot Rehabilitation Centre, the place that was to be my home for several months. Unlike the prestigious Dalcross Hospital, Talbot was a squat yellow-brick building in a nondescript suburb, surrounded by concrete car parks and bounded by busy roads. In my mind I'd built up my return to Melbourne, but now my heart sank. Mum and Dad wheeled me into the eerily silent reception area. I sensed their nervousness at handing me over to strangers, but also their hope that here I would somehow be transformed back into the Old Em. Although I was warmed by that optimism, deep down I feared that I was too broken to fix.

My parents cautiously steered me down what felt like endless empty corridors, following the signs to the Mellor unit, the neurological ward where I was to be rehabilitated. I felt sick and dizzy from the short wheelchair ride and utterly exhausted from the huge day of travelling. We finally approached a dated, fluoro-lit nurses' station. From my wheelchair perspective all I could see was the worn green lino floor. Above me Dad chatted to a bubbly nurse and signed forms. My admission sorted, the nurse seized control of my wheelchair. The wheels shrieked against the shiny lino and I moaned at the sudden speed as she rushed me down more corridors to my room. I could hear my parents' footsteps behind us as they hurried to keep up.

In the room were four identical beds, and the empty one with the *Welcome Em* sign, courtesy of a thoughtful friend, was clearly mine. The nurse briskly lifted me into it, saying, "Best if, Mum and Dad, you leave and let Emma get used to her new room." Mum's eyes welled up with tears and she kissed me on the cheek. "See you tomorrow, my Em," she said reassuringly. Dad put his hand on my shoulder, squeezed it and got out his keys. They left.

I felt as though I had been thrown into gaol. The nurse whipped off my shoes, threw up my bed's sides and said, "Rest now, Dear. Dinner's at 5pm and your buzzer's here should you need anything. You'll meet your therapists tomorrow."

After the hotel-like accommodation in the Sydney hospital, I was now forced to share a room with three other patients, strangers. Strangers who would be apparently returning soon, but I wasn't particularly looking forward to meeting. All alone for the moment, I scanned the room through the thin blue nylon curtain that was my only privacy. The furniture was cloned – same beds, same bedside tables, identical narrow chipboard lockers. At least I was next to the window, but the view was far from inspiring – a bleak car park and in the distance an industrial brick chimney. I felt abandoned in an alien world.

Resigned, I collapsed back on the hard squeaky pillows. With no distractions, I felt forced to focus on my situation and all the things that were not right or fair about it. Endless negative issues circled in my damaged mind. I felt like I'd been dumped at Talbot's doorstep, a complex machine with no manual. The discharge summary from Dalcross provided the new Talbot staff with a 'problem list'. Now it was their job to write the manual.

At Talbot my days changed dramatically. In my Sydney hospital I had been allowed to stay in bed in my pyjamas and everyone did everything for me. My world was now controlled by the routine of the hospital. Each day started with a painful burst of light as Nurse Fran threw up the blind and wound up my bed, bringing my crooked prone body to a crooked seated position. Breakfast in bed, once a treat, was now a chore. I was given a shaving mirror to help me eat. It was embarrassing to admit that I'd even forgotten where my mouth was. Looking at my reflection, though, was enough to put me into famine mode! Attempts at feeding myself were hopeless. Puree everywhere but in my mouth. No wonder my shower was always timetabled after breakfast! *I needed a baby's plastic floor protector.*

Fran arrives, quickly transfers me to the commode chair and wheels me into the toilet, then rushes off without realising that the chair hasn't been positioned right over the bowl. Like a little kid I totally miss.

I reach for the buzzer, buzz, and wait.

About ten minutes later I buzz again. Fran flies in out of breath, "Sorry Em, another nurse needed a hand. Are you finished?"

"Yeaaahh ut," I try to let her know what's happened. She looks down and sees the wet floor.

"Oh dear. My fault Em, sorry!" She pushes me out of the way and mops up.

"OK. Now for your shower." I'm wheeled into the shower recess and rapidly lathered and hosed down. The commode chair is pinching my skin but I can't tell her. I can't even move to cover myself. I'm acutely aware of how vulnerable I am. The reality of my new helpless self hits me hard, like a slap in the face. I'm coming down way too quickly from the medication cloud I've existed in since the operation.

Fran dries me off and struggles me into the clothes she's pulled from my drawer – knickers, bra, trackies, Ted pressure stockings and shoes. I feel I'm being forced to squeeze my new disabled body into my old grey tracksuit.

I try to let her know telepathically that she's forgotten to do up my bra, but she fails to get that message. She then adopts a 'will you marry me' position and attempts to cram my left foot into my right shoe. She stops, huffs, gets down on both knees and tries again.

Another voice calls for Fran's assistance so I'm wheeled shoeless to face the wall rather than the window and instructed to wait. I still have to have my teeth cleaned and shoes put on before Susan, the porter, comes to take me to my scheduled assessments for the day. *I'm dead tired already.* Even though I feel as though a concrete fatigue fog is squashing me, I don't want to rest. I want to start fixing my body. *Now*. If I could physically throw a tantrum, I would.

~

Talbot consisted of two different areas, the therapy area where I was to be 'fixed' and the ward where I would sleep or rest and wait in between. Susan manoeuvred my chair easily with one hand across the glass-arched walkway that bridged these two new worlds. When my wheelchair tyres left the green lino floor of the ward and were pushed onto the parquetry floor and more natural light of the therapy wing, my spirits rose. Past the café and with a 'knock knock knock' I was delivered like a parcel to my first assessment. Before any therapy could begin I had to have my 'admission level of disability' determined by a swarm of new therapists from each discipline – from physio to OT to speech therapy to psych.

As a therapist I knew that a strong therapeutic foundation was crucial to elicit a person's strengths, motivation and sustain their performance. But as a patient I suddenly felt myself very closed to those who robotically assessed me, assuming that I, the patient, would have nothing to contribute to the process. I needed to feel valued before I could reciprocate and build any rapport with them.

It seemed that not one of my newly acquired 'stroke-induced' deficits was straightforward. The problem list was way longer and more extensive than I or they had thought. The bleeding in my right cerebellum affected the right side of my face and the left side of my body. I couldn't sit or stand upright, so restoring my balance was a priority. Bed or wheelchair-bound, I now existed in a topsy-turvy spinning world where everything was double. As well as feeling perpetually dizzy, any movement was made worse by the nerve damage from the stroke. My left side felt like it had been dipped in hot wax, lifeless and stiff but with raging nerve pain trapped inside. As I couldn't close my right eye, it was taped shut to allow me single vision. The right side of my face drooped. I had no sense of my body in space, where my mouth, eyes or fingers were. Basically at this point I couldn't sit up, turn my head, point, blink, talk or eat anything other than thickened fluids.

These new deficits made me disabled, trapped and categorised. I felt handicapped, an aberration. But at the same time, I felt ashamed to admit that this bothered me. *As an OT surely I should've been familiar with and accepting of my situation?*

I was eligible for almost everything on offer at Talbot, from physio to psych. A rehab timetable was plastered above my bed, with sessions beginning every day at 9am and going through till 4.30pm. The timetable included regular rest times but I didn't want those. I was there to work.

Chapter 21
Therapy Begins

I started the various sessions full of optimism and high expectations, with no idea how slow and repetitive the process was going to be, or how emotionally draining. It was fairly naïve of me, considering I was a therapist, but probably indicative of the gulf that exists between the mindset of the therapist and that of the patient.

To get to therapy, I had to get my wheels sorted. That was the job of the OT, Felicity. I had to be fitted for a special high-backed wheelchair to support my weak neck, upper limb and back muscles. The OT also had to give me a shower assessment, a standard tool used by my profession to find out a person's capabilities and areas to be improved. I'd done plenty of them but had never been at the receiving end. Sitting naked, propped up in a shower chair, in front of a colleague my age, was deeply humiliating.

"Try to sit upright," Felicity said encouragingly as I sat slumped under the running water. I knew she was trying to help but I just felt like slipping down the drain hole. *Had I really put others through this excruciating experience? Surely my profession was there to empower people not disempower them?* After proving I couldn't shower myself I then had to prove I couldn't dress myself. Even though it was patently obvious I could do nothing for myself at that stage, the medical bureaucracy required these assessments to be done before any therapy could proceed.

Once that was over I could begin my twice-daily physiotherapy regime. The physio area was a huge, cold room like a carpentry workshop, bordered by rows of blue vinyl beds where patients were being worked on. I'd imagined I'd be running in no time, but the reality was I'd be spending my first few months there on the sidelines.

"Today we're going to work on straightening you up," my physio, Georgie, announced enthusiastically. My nickname was 'Lamana Banana' because even when I lay flat I curved like a banana. One of the first exercises involved me lying on my back while Georgie coaxed my bent body into a straight line. It was a weird and quite frightening feeling. Being curved felt safe.

Then she rocked me from side to side to give me a sense of what it would feel like to sit up. The bleed had caused muscle amnesia and these small slow movements were a way of rousing them again.

"Blink, Em," Georgie would say. I heard and understood, but it took at least five seconds for my right eyelid to obey. Even then it would only go down halfway, like a broken blind.

"All done today, Em." Suddenly the 25-minute session would be over. I couldn't believe it. Progress was agonisingly slow. All I'd done was blink and try to stretch out straight, and I was exhausted. As I sat waiting to be returned to my room to rest, I watched other patients enviously. Some were grasping their way along the eight-metre practice set of parallel bars down the middle of the room. That was where I wanted to be, but I was beginning to realise what a long road lay ahead.

Between sessions I was wheeled back across the glass bridge to the other side to rest. These sleep times to 'rest and heal' were far from restful. My roommates had visitors or the cleaners banged and crashed about. I'd lie awake, unable to move to toss and turn. I'd often head off to the next session feeling grumpy and irritable, and worried that I wouldn't perform at my best.

Speech therapy was held in a tiny shoebox of a room. It overlooked Talbot's central garden courtyard but *my* view was of my eye-patched self. My wheelchair would be positioned by Nancy, my therapist, in front of a large mirror so I could track my facial movements. In the early stages, though, there were no movements to track. I had to relearn how to move my frozen lopsided face and wake the muscles involved. I had no sense of where anything was – my tongue, my eyes, my mouth. Communication consisted of trying to move my face in a meaningful way and emitting muffled sounds. The voice that did escape at that stage was monotonous and incomprehensible, and came out startlingly loud or invisibly soft. I sounded like a robot with its volume dial out of control.

The first few speech therapy sessions didn't change much. I would spend the whole session repetitively trying to poke out my tongue, or pursing my lips together and then stretching them to produce the sounds *oo* and *ee*. It was bad enough doing such things in front of Nancy, but at one of these sessions a male student was invited in to observe. They did ask my permission but I could hardly refuse, since he was already standing there, plus my ability to say "No" was pretty compromised at that stage. I didn't feel as though I had a choice. As a therapist I knew it was standard clinical practice to let students observe, but now I realised how disempowering and embarrassing it was being on the other side of it.

Measuring my smile (with an Ikea tape measure) was another part of the routine. Even though after weeks it was still hardly a smirk, every millimetre I managed to stretch my mouth elicited a cry of encouragement from Nancy. *Baby steps!* At least I had moved on from the communication board I had relied on at Dalcross.

Gathering feedback, whether it was recording my voice, tracking my handwriting, taking photos of my face or videos of my walking became a huge motivation to me. In spite of the slowness of my recovery, it helped me track small changes and show others that I was still improving. I knew too as a therapist that seeing this feedback would be great to show my future team. Showing that I couldn't speak or hold up my head through real recorded examples would be much more powerful than just using words to describe my recovery process.

An early therapy I was really looking forward to was 'hydro' or warm water therapy. I secretly clung to the hope that the water would wash away my disability and my balance would be miraculously restored. First, though, I needed to improve my breathing and swallowing, as my medical team feared I would aspirate if I entered the water. So as well as my speech regime I was sent to music therapy. *Yep, I had to sing to swim.*

Music sessions were held in an incense-fragrant room, full of instruments, colour and comfy cushions. The window looked out on a pleasant view of gum trees. In my former life as an OT I'd regarded music therapy as a bit of a 'time filler' but I soon learnt these sessions have surprising physical and emotional benefits.

My body had basically forgotten how to breathe and at first I could only hold a note for less than a second. The music therapist, Tina, would sit at the piano and play a note and sing and I would try to copy her. I sounded awful and I mentally added 'can't sing' to the long list of what I *couldn't* do, but slowly the exercises restored some breath control and endurance.

At the end of a day of therapy, I would feel exhausted but still had a mass of 'homework' to do before my visitors arrived. It wasn't compulsory, but I was determined to improve, whether it was working on my balance by standing at my cot-sides in five-, ten- or 15-minute intervals, or practising syllables in speech.

After a few weeks of therapy I was scheduled to attend my first family meeting. In my previous role as an OT, such meetings had been a weekly occurrence, so I felt I knew what to expect. But being the focus of the gathering was a big eye-opener for me.

Basically, my new team and parents gathered sardine-like around a large wooden table. I was wheeled in and positioned at the top. A doctor to my left led the meeting. Clockwise we then heard from the other eight or so staff (and their students) about my progress, where I'd come from, and the numerous goals of each discipline. It was a cruel reminder of the devastating spot I was in and the limitations each discipline had put on me. When it came around to my parents they were asked if they had any questions. 'No' is all they said. *Why had I attended? No one asked me for my thoughts. What a wasted opportunity.* My entire team had been together in one room, the ideal chance to brainstorm meaningful goals together and draw on my strengths and values to achieve these. *Surely my treatment plan should be based on a list of what I could do?* My family could have also been educated then and there and perhaps they too would've felt included in my team and empowered to care for me in the future.

Although I started the various therapy sessions full of optimism, I discovered new disabilities every day. The more activity I did, the more disabilities appeared. They were made worse by my immense fatigue and the growing frustration at my slow progress. I was finding just how disabled my body really was.

Chapter 22
Three Months on – the Rehab Roller-coaster

I'd arrived at Talbot in mid-winter. By spring I was deemed medically fit enough to be able to propel my own wheelchair, which gave me a touch more freedom. In between sessions I'd exit the dark and gloomy life of the ward where my fellow patients were resting on their beds and wheel myself towards the 'therapy zone'. Here, I'd park my wheelchair in the natural light and warmth of the glass walkway. If I positioned my chair at an angle, I could see the tin roof and treetops in the distance, a glimpse of the outside world while still safe behind the glass.

Although I had improved I was still having trouble keeping up with Talbot. It was a fast-moving, efficient place, because they wanted me to be independent, but sometimes their careless actions and brisk attitude had the opposite effect.

Whether it was forgetting to shut the bathroom door and revealing my naked body to the world, asking me if I'd like a Malteser when I couldn't eat chocolate or swallow properly, failing to put the bed brakes on, or giving me a 'wedgie' while holding the back of my pants when walking me, there were numerous incidents during my stay that reinforced my feelings of dependency and powerlessness. I'm sure these actions were not intentional, but in my AVM victim mentality I saw them as such. Already feeling vulnerable and defeated, I became fairly cynical about the treatment I was receiving, and that cynicism certainly didn't help speed up my recovery.

In rehab I needed help with just about everything, but hated asking for it. Some people seemed to make the whole process rather difficult. At times the staff seemed too busy to attend to my needs or would frequently avoid eye contact to save time. I remember in about my second week of rehab the first time I really tried to communicate with one of my doctors. He was walking down the corridor on my ward at the end of the day, carrying a pile of notes. I couldn't call out or wave my arms about to get his attention, so I fixed my eyes in his direction. I knew he could see me, but he was busy reading the notes so he kept looking down and continued walking. I know I have done the same myself as a therapist, but the impact his behaviour had on me that day, when I already felt so stripped of all other means of communicating, was huge. I felt so forgotten, like an odd sock. Powerless. If he'd said, "Em, I'll see you tomorrow," that would have been fine. The disregard I received that day really made me see how powerful communication is and how simple things like eye contact and body language can really impact your relationships and recovery.

There are so many small humiliations in the hospital day. Simple things like eating were suddenly immensely complicated, juggling the tasks of cutting food, getting it to my mouth accurately and then chewing and swallowing it. It wasn't a pretty sight and holding a conversation was quite impossible if a visitor arrived. I often went hungry. At least eating alone in bed gave me the freedom to be messy. When at last I graduated to the dining room I found myself surrounded by grandmotherly conversations and felt self-conscious about my eating style.

❧

At 5pm sharp I'm seated in a low chair. From this height I try to eat the mashed potato and pea meal in front of me. I spend the first 15 minutes chasing my peas around with my fork, mouth wide open in case I capture one. Both hungry and embarrassed at my endless failed attempts, I put down my cutlery and to the other elderly ladies' horror, I use my fingers to pick up the green escape artists and stuff them into my mash. It was either forget etiquette or die from frustration, starvation or dizziness after circling my plate countless times.

❧

I wasn't the only one who had problems in the dining room. Another patient who'd had a stroke was Mel, but she had no physical signs. She had no problem feeding herself but her word-finding difficulties made mealtimes a challenge. "What would ya like, Sweetie-Pie?" the nurse once asked, wheeling around a trolley of green jellies, cheesecake and ice-cream.

"I'll have cheese cake and lipstick," Mel said.

The nurse, perplexed, corrected her. "You mean cheesecake and ice-cream don't you?"

Mel's conversations were broken with pauses of frustration while she tried to articulate the name of an object or a word that was on the tip of her tongue. While I also had immense trouble communicating, it wasn't due to not knowing what to say. It was merely that I had to relearn how to say it.

Medication was as much a routine part of my day as meals at Talbot. Because I was in constant pain I became the guinea pig for every possible pain medication, but none succeeded in touching even the edge of my raw nerve pain. The medications only seemed to produce unpleasant side effects. Some made my dizziness worse, others caused nausea, and then I would be prescribed yet another to mask that side effect. For example, when I became dizzy I was given Maxolon. The intention seemed to be to cover any symptom that would stop me going to therapy.

Although it was a tough period, small pleasures were slowly returning to my life. I started to take an interest in my appearance again. I'd always had a lot of respect for people who tried to look their best despite their physical disability. They appeared to have not 'surrendered'. Now I needed to show that I wasn't giving up either. One of my best friends, a nail technician, brought her box of nail tools and polished and transformed my nails regularly. It was so therapeutic having a non-invasive, non-medical procedure that I decided it was time to book an appointment with the hospital hairdresser. She would come to us on the ward and temporarily occupy one of the storage rooms. I was hoping that the familiar soothing experience of having my hair washed would bring a little normality back into my life and boost my self-image.

~

When I wheel up to my appointment there isn't the usual, "How would you like it today, Em?" … "Look at these mags to get an idea" or "Would you like a coffee?" Instead the hairdresser just handles my clumps of hair distastefully as if to say, "What on earth can I do with this?" She gives me a three-minute dry cut.

"There we go, now just walk over to the sink behind you and we'll wash it," she says, in a bored tone. *I can't walk over there, I think. If I could walk, I'd walk out of here and to another salon!*

But I swallow my frustration and wheel myself towards the sink. "Now just put your head forward."

I do, dizzy.

"No, no, Emma. I said back." She flips my head back 180 degrees like a toilet seat.

My tender skull slams against the ceramic sink.

I leave the 'salon' feeling like a shorn sheep. She's chopped off my hair and hacked my self-esteem even more brutally.

~

At least my speech was improving and I could debrief and joke a little with my visitors about such experiences. I still had lots of visitors and support, although there were some friends who just sent cards and kept their distance. It was hard not to take this personally, but I assumed they found my new situation too confronting to deal with.

Each day at 4.30pm sharp, Mum and Dad would arrive, greeting me with a hug, bearing a take-away coffee for them and a small cup of lukewarm 'bubbacino' (froth but no chocolate) for me. Although my speech therapist had said "No" to hot and thin fluids, I could eat the cold white froth and each spoonful was magic. The familiarity of the coffee ritual and their presence was priceless. It was the only thing in that phase that I felt they too could enjoy. That we could enjoy together.

But at the same time I felt that they were wasting their time, money and effort. They could never replace all that had been taken from me. This stroke had wrecked my life. I didn't want it to destroy their lives too.

"What have you done today, Em?" Dad would ask.

"Rehab," I'd reply in a flat voice. *What was I meant to say to them? That I could now follow a moving finger with my eyes without moving my head*. In my mind, I had nothing to show other than utter exhaustion for the immense effort I put into my therapy each day.

When my friends or family came unannounced to my therapy sessions I felt completely humiliated. Having them cheer from the sidelines while I stacked cones or threw quoits only made me feel disappointed for them that my recovery was so slow. Although I definitely needed their support, at the same time their presence seemed to make me feel so reliant on them. They did for me what I had to learn to do for myself. On the other hand the Talbot staff were always making me do things independently, so when my close family and friends visited, I'd feel so shattered I'd let them take over. I needed a break and it was a relief to be able to drop my guard in their company.

In October 2005, my close friends and family organised a fundraiser called 'RUN to GEE' where over a hundred of my supporters ran or walked to my rehabilitation facility to raise funds for Talbot and show their support. Even friends overseas at the time organised a London version. They all (even my dog!) wore specially designed blue t-shirts reading 'RUN to GEE 'cos we're inspired'. Registration forms, course maps, sponsorship letters and invitations were produced.

An information brochure distributed to those who participated read:

"Em loves to run and months before she was diagnosed with an AVM, she trained for a half-marathon – but this would pale in comparison to her preparation for the next marathon she would be running. At just 24 years of age she prepared her will and said goodbye to all those that she loved. Though she recovered from surgery, she spent months in hospital learning to walk again. Not only did Em continue to be incredibly selfless in supporting her friends and family through their own distress but, as an occupational therapist, Emma created the possibility for herself to be 'inspirational and courageous' in her recovery and to one day return to work as a better and more client-centred therapist. We continue to watch in awe as Em runs the biggest marathon of her life. Every day she teaches us not to ask 'why me?' but 'how can I best get through this?" Only a few things in life teach us that, which is why we are running … a small marathon of thanks from us all … We want to motivate Emma in her recovery by showing her just how much she means to us and how inspired we are."

Although at the time I wasn't well enough to attend the event, to this day the swarm of peoples' efforts is proof of the support that has fuelled my recovery.

In fact, after getting to know fellow patients, like Dean, I realised how lucky I was to have family and friends around. Dean was from New South Wales and had been admitted following a stroke on a business trip to Melbourne. He looked like Mr Bean – pasty white, hairy skin and dark eyes. One afternoon I saw him sitting peering vaguely out the dining-room window. I had 15 minutes before my visitors arrived so I decided to wheel over.

"U 'K?" I mumbled, thinking he was probably wondering how a mute, eye-patched young girl on wheels could help. I can't talk very well, but I can still listen, I thought.

"Not really," he said, resting his chin on his right palm. His left arm was flaccid and lay awkwardly across his thighs. "Basically I've been working crazy hours. It was lucky I had my stroke on a business trip. I live alone in Sydney and I doubt my secretary would check up on me."

"Fam mi ly?" I asked haltingly.

"My sister's in Brisbane and we're not that close. No other family. My parents passed away years ago."

"Frens?" I posed hopefully.

"Nup, not really." His chin dropped further to his torso, seemingly heavy. He slowly shook his head from side to side, fixing his teary eyes in the direction of his knees.

I wheeled my chair closer and placed my hand on his sunken left shoulder. We sat in silence until my friends arrived and I sheepishly left.

Although I was lucky to have so many visitors, an awkwardness hung in the air. We were all tentatively trying to work out our new roles. Many of my close family and friends are from a medical background and, because of this, the hospital team tended to assume they would know how to deal with my recovery. But my supporters found it increasingly hard to emotionally detach themselves from what was happening to me. They couldn't be merely observers or advisors.

My stroke had changed everything. I was not the same person or friend in the relationship that family and friends had committed to. Now they were also my carers and were torn between that and who they'd always been to me over the last 24 years.

As my mum wrote later, "I needed to learn new ways to relate to my daughter. She didn't want pity or patronising behaviours yet I pitied her and I patronised and I did things for her that she wanted and needed to do for herself. I was treading on eggshells and yet neither of us wanted that at all. I spent my time with her *doing* the many things that needed doing when often what she wanted/needed more was for me to sit with her, to listen to her, to share with her."

As time passed, I sensed the dilemma I had forced upon those close to me. I tried to be positive and strong for their sake, but at the same time felt utterly terrified of losing them. *Would they stick around when they realised that the 'Old Em' wasn't returning?* I wanted to reciprocate their acts of friendship, but being physically trapped, this was near impossible.

It became easy to hide behind my eye patch. If I was tired, people would understand. I had plenty of physical reasons to support my fatigued state and excuse my grumpy behaviour. I admit to often blaming those close to me or finding fault in what they did, merely to escape responsibility. I daily questioned their amazing investment in my wellbeing. I tried to dismiss these thoughts and in those 'survival days' I became reliant on others' comments to get my depleted self-esteem through each day. *Were their words just said out of niceness or habit? What were they really thinking?*

All I longed for was to be my old independent self, but I stubbornly wouldn't take therapists' advice on ways to manage my pain and conserve my energy. Of course I knew the importance of such strategies, but I wanted to keep doing things the same way I'd always done them. After a full day of pushing through my exhaustion I would just fall in a frustrated, irritable heap.

Rehab became a perilous journey where I was forced to spend each day working on my disabilities while stubbornly refusing to accept them, or to contemplate any reference to stroke. *I was an AVM victim. Strokes were for older people, unfit people and unhealthy people. I was none of these.* Volunteer stroke survivors would come and speak to us about their experiences and how, "having a stroke was the best thing that had happened to them". I'd be forced to observe my invited family members' relief at the stroke survivor's words. I was glad someone else could give them hope, but I just felt ungrateful and alone. I didn't want to identify with this man, or any of the other stroke victims I found myself with.

I was silently consumed by negative, self-pitying thoughts. In my mind I was there because of an unfortunate accident, whereas I felt that in some way their situations were self-inflicted. They smoked or lived unhealthy lifestyles, like my roommate Sandy, a peroxided-blonde in her mid-40s. Her husky voice was a dead giveaway that her 'ciggies' were an essential part of her daily regime. Although she did add life and energy to the room, when she limped out on her stick for 'smoko' I would inwardly struggle. I hated that she would return to her previous unhealthy lifestyle smoking 50 a day and I also confess to being jealous of her early discharge from the ward. She almost ran out of the place, something which, after months of rehabilitation myself, I was still unable to do.

The truth was I was totally unprepared for the emotional impact my stroke would have on my life. Although I still had my marbles, the endless physical disabilities that emerged, and the frustration of not being able to communicate meant that these marbles only smashed around uselessly inside my damaged head. I clung onto the idea of returning to my old life. But as time went by, the realisation sunk in that my past identity had vanished when I'd had my stroke. *Everything I once was good at was now gone. I'm useless!*

There were days when I just didn't feel motivated to start another day putting my disabled body through the paces. But on these rare occasions, I struggled to stop and grieve, as I felt bombarded by my team. They'd ask probing questions. "Why don't you feel like going to physio today, Em?" or suggest antidepressants to mask the emotional hindrance they could see was affecting my physical progress.

To escape their hassling and to avoid being prescribed medication I dreaded, I would go to the scheduled session, but not be present. Just extremely frustrated that I couldn't give it 100 per cent. I felt as though I needed a break. *Surely it was normal for me to grieve*. Acknowledging and balancing my emotional and physical progression was becoming increasingly difficult.

I realised the only way out was to rebuild my confidence and somehow find a new identity. *I had a choice*. I could sit and sulk or do what I was there to do – get rehabilitated. *I had to choose to be proactive in my recovery rather than reactive. I had to change my attitude.*

Chapter 23
Mid-therapy – Baby Steps

At the far end of the room was a mirror and my bent-over reflection stared at me as I inched along. It was meant to be there as a form of feedback, to correct my posture, but it was hardly motivating.

After months of physio, I was out of my wheelchair and walking with the aid of a frame. But it was no quick transition. I had to practise with 12 bricks in my frame's basket, to stabilise it and weigh me down. One by one the bricks were being removed as my body control and endurance improved, until I could hold my body up and wasn't as much of a 'Lamana Banana' if I concentrated.

One day Felicity, the OT, and Georgie, the physio, worked together and we headed outside so I could learn to negotiate uneven surfaces with my frame. I'd been looking forward to getting out into the fresh air and the sun, but after months of life behind glass, it was a bit daunting. There were sticky flies, loose pebbles and even the wind threw my delicate balance. In spite of the obstacles we were all having a lot of fun, even though laughing made me shake and added an extra challenge to my already wobbly walking. Felicity swatted flies and held my billowing top down, while Georgie guided my frame over speed humps.

Having different disciplines working together like this was a treat. Even though a team approach is seen as ideal in theory, the reality of the medical world means therapists generally tend to work within the 'silos' of their own disciplines. As a patient that day I felt at the centre of their care, that they were working together *with* me rather than *for* me.

My music therapist, Tina, also sometimes teamed up with my physio. In music therapy I'd graduated from scales to singing along (badly) to songs. Tina encouraged me to choose songs with lyrics that meant something to me. Missy Higgins' 'Nightminds' was a particular favourite. The words *I will learn to breathe this ugliness you see* still give me chills. The lyrics I heard somehow helped me reconnect with and express trapped emotions. Relearning to sing was also curiously effective in restoring my speech patterns. Music therapy opened up a whole new world for me. Music became a great comfort and another source of independence. Listening to my iPod out of therapy hours became quite an escape.

When Tina came to the gym she would play guitar as Georgie and I marched to the rhythm. While it was a little embarrassing being serenaded and caused a bit of laughter among other patients, moving to a rhythm definitely helped my walking. Once again, two therapists working together felt far more effective than seeing them individually.

At speech therapy I would sit in front of the now-familiar mirror while Jacqui, the speech therapy assistant, sat to one side with her clipboard on her lap. I was now used to watching my own facial gymnastics and had more control over my tongue and jaw. My speaking was slowly becoming more comprehensible through repeating individual syllables over and over.

~

"Puh, puh, puh." I'd been concentrating furiously on the list of sounds in front of me and Jacqui's facial examples. I'd finally forced my unwilling lips together. She clapped. "Excellent! Now let's try to put it in a word. See if you can say *Peter Pan*, Em."

I appreciate her enthusiasm but I feel like I'm in Playschool. The words are meaningless.

"Eeter Aan," I say. The lips won't behave this time. It comes out all wrong. *Great*, I think to myself sarcastically.

"Put your lips together like this."

I watch her and try. "Eeter Aan." My second attempt is just as bad.

"That's better," exclaims Jacqui, though we both know it was exactly the same, if not clumsier than last time.

Tears well up in my left eye, but I don't have time to mope. *I have 20 minutes left to get my p's sounding like p's.*

"You're tired aren't you, Em?" says Jacqui sympathetically. "A few more and then we'll finish up."

I bring the photocopied list of words closer. "Eeter, aan, paan." The lips come together at last. "Paan." I stop to catch my breath and we smile at each other triumphantly. *Man, I've just said the letter P and we're both acting as if I've just finished a 20-kilometre run!*

Jacqui places a red plastic folder on my lap, full of 'p' words to practise saying, "Only if you feel up to it, Em."

~

Months of daily speech therapy and weekly music therapy had my swallowing mechanisms working better and at last I was ready for swimming. My brand-new black one-piece bathers and Speedo goggles could finally be christened.

At hydro, instead of diving or bombing I would wait in my wheelchair behind two supervisors. Here, no one worried about body shapes or bikini lines. Depending on your ability, you were either lifted by a machine or supported to walk into the murky warm water. The advantage of hydro was that in the water balance wouldn't be a problem and I would be able to do things I couldn't possibly do on land. I'd been looking forward to this moment for months, and I was devastated to find I couldn't even stand upright in the water. Its warmth just heightened my fatigue and my nerve pain, making the left side of my body feel dead and heavy. Instead of feeling buoyant and free, I felt like a ship's anchor.

I was destined to spend months walking slowly along the pool edge or clutching a therapist. By the end of my time in hydro I could move alone into the deep end and float, huge achievements in my now limited realm. Water therapy was slow going but very important. Being able to move my limbs freely gave me physical confidence and restored a sense of freedom and independence.

OT had begun badly with my naked shower session. But now I'd built a good friendship with my therapist, Felicity, and was fully dressed. These sessions were scheduled daily after lunch and involved small physical tasks designed to improve my motor skills, dexterity and function.

OT was the most challenging therapy for me. More than in any of the other therapies, I found my role reversal hard to accept.

Despite Felicity's understanding, it felt really wrong being a therapist in therapy. My professional knowledge made me over-analytical and a little cynical. I knew the clinical reasoning behind these activities and their role in returning a person to some kind of meaningful activity, but with my patient's eyes I saw how demeaning and monotonous some tasks could be.

At times a peg-board was placed in front of me, and I'd be left to move wooden pegs from hole to hole, or I'd be given a pile of handwriting sheets and asked to trace letter after letter as if I was a Grade One student. The best sessions were meaningful, little projects like making chess pieces and chopping boards. I enjoyed relearning how to bake and assemble gingerbread houses, which I'd always done pre-stroke at Christmas. Here, I was working with another person and there was an outcome, something to show my visitors to prove my daily therapy efforts were worthwhile.

But, as in all sessions, things moved far too slowly for my liking. I became very frustrated in OT. I hated my 'old-lady' walking frame; I called it Anchovy because I hate anchovies. Rather than wait for the OT to go through all the red tape of organising a funkier new frame, I arranged it myself. I also began to design my own therapy, trialling strategies to adapt to my new physical self. One example was the use of a glove to minimise the growing nerve pain in my left hand. Possibly these strategies were ones that Felicity had already mentioned but I hadn't been ready to adopt in my unreceptive frame of mind.

Felicity patiently discussed future goals, like my intention to return to work and move out of home. I have to admit I was never fully present in these conversations. I was not prepared to be taking advice from someone in my own profession. I remained in denial that life outside the Talbot walls would be any different to the way it had been. I continued to stubbornly believe that I still had my old job, an extremely supportive workplace and my silver manual car waiting for me.

Over time, Felicity managed to thread purpose, meaning and value back into my life. Initially these discussions were quite daunting and made me think about the realities of my future.

~

"So Em, how are you feeling about leaving here and going back to work?" Felicity asks.

"K," I'd lie, resting my head on the back of my high-backed wheelchair so it didn't wobble so much.

"So what are the bits in your old job that'd be a bit tricky for a while?" Felicity gently probes.

My mind fast-forwards through my old typical working life as an OT. I skip my early run and get straight to getting to work. Driving there. Walking from the car park to the department. Talking. Typing … and that's just the admin stuff! How could I make a hand splint to help a patient to grasp when I struggled using my own hand and no longer could feel the hot temperature of the wax? How could I lift and carry a piece of equipment to help them?

"Every bit," I grunt, resigned.

"OK, let's brainstorm together what you love about your job and go from there …" Felicity says enthusiastically, poising her pen to catch the list.

~

As time went on, the holistic and empowering nature of OT rekindled my love for the profession. Today, I am so grateful that Felicity put up with my cynical, stubborn behaviour.

The various physical therapies began to show results, so I was booked in for 'psych'. One of my fellow patients, Ida, who had become a kind of grandmother figure to me, had survived a stroke during an operation. She was very wary of psych sessions or anything of that nature and was horrified when she heard where I was going. "It's ridiculous. You've had a stroke but you're not loopy," she huffed.

Although I didn't feel 'loopy', I understood the importance of addressing the emotional issues that piggybacked any physical ones. Off I went to the fourth floor, where the seaweed-green carpet led to the quiet, dark and musty psych department.

Denise, my psychologist, was a softly spoken, middle-aged woman who seemed nervous in my company. I didn't have these sessions often, and when I did I largely felt like a zoo animal as she watched me, trying to elicit the trapped emotions that my speech wouldn't allow me to unleash.

"How do you feel today?" Denise would ask.

After a few minutes of awkward silence, she'd glance at her wristwatch, seemingly bored. She was probably just checking the time, but in my vulnerable state I'd take Denise's aloof behaviour personally.

She'd move on with the questions, talking me through the 'stages of grief' with no feedback from me.

"Are you frustrated, Em? Tell me how you feel."

Yes of course I'm frustrated and I can't begin to convey to you how I feel. If I could yell and scream what's trapped inside I would! I thought angrily, unable to find a way to respond in the brief pause before she continued, "It's OK to be frustrated."

Psych was indeed frustrating and rarely included in my regime, but as my communication improved it did help. I took her advice and with her and others' assistance resumed my diary writing, keeping a journal. It proved to be a good emotional outlet, a way to let off steam.

I now wish more attention had been paid to the emotional aftermath of my stroke. The 12 bricks I carted around in physio seemed nothing compared to the mental load I was lugging around. Realistically I couldn't have survived my stroke without being emotionally scathed. Any physical trauma impacts you and those around you emotionally. Improving my plummeting self-esteem and reinventing my identity was crucial to allow me to endure the physical battle that lay ahead. It would be a long time before I could begin to accept what I couldn't change about my new self, and try to change what I could.

Chapter 24
Leaving Talbot

By summer I had joined my fellow patients, walking on the parallel bars down the middle of the physio room. I could shuffle my wobbly body around in a full circle in 30 seconds and even began using my frame to walk to the various sessions. I still needed a wheelchair for long distances and when outside Talbot, but the number of bricks in my frame's basket had been gradually reduced. I'd also graduated to the gym and had replaced my rest breaks with sessions with the exercise physiologist, Gary, who somehow made exercising fun. The gym equipment was old, but to me it was gold. Exercise had always been a great stress release for me, and this glimpse of independence meant some escape from the bubble I'd been trapped in for months. *Freedom!* When the therapy area closed at 4.30pm each day and I had to reluctantly return to the ward, I'd feel totally exhausted and overwhelmed with how far I still had to go, but felt I couldn't afford to stop. After my visitors left each night, I'd do laps of the ward on my frame, trying to get my restless body moving and restless mind to settle.

It was a time of milestones. I was even able to return to my coffee fix. After months of consuming thickened fluids and puree, I had progressively relearnt to drink and swallow better, eventually able to tolerate my favourite beverage. But even that task had to be modified. My inability to decipher hot from cold meant that I had to drink my cappuccino with a straw from a thermo cup.

This made the Talbot cafeteria a good escape for me. Rather than sit in my room or join the other patients for their smokos, I would opt to sit among the buzz of the café. I'd order a lukewarm coffee, slurp it through a straw, and read Don't Give Up-style motivational books, searching for a remedy for my low self-esteem and trying to face my latest fear – leaving Talbot.

Now that my condition was more stable I had already returned to my parents' home occasionally for a weekend. It was something I looked forward to, as therapy was non-existent at Talbot on the weekend. The therapists went home, the gym was locked, the metal roller doors barred my now daily order from the cafeteria and the fluorescent lights of the therapy zone were switched off.

At least at home I was able to soak up 48 hours of TLC and rest. But having Mum shower me and my dad give me my stingy Clexane injections wasn't what I'd imagined. I tried hard not to get frustrated and discouraged by this dependence. I had to focus on the things I could now do, to regain some control over this disability that had invaded my body. To not be the burden that I felt I had become.

I'd sometimes clear the lunch table for Mum.

"You don't have to do that, Em," she would say, grabbing the dishes off my unsteady frame and putting them in the sink.

I'd want to say, 'I know I don't have to, but I want to and I can!' But all that came out was, "I can. Ma."

In spite of my efforts to feel useful when staying with Mum and Dad, I realised they couldn't sustain their upbeat attitudes when I was around 24/7. It was a taste of the future. By the end of each weekend I sensed that my family were dreading my permanent return and seemed relieved to let others care for me for a while. At the same time I'd become institutionalised and after two days away from the *centre I longed to be boomeranged back to the safety of the place where I felt now strangely more at home and accepted.* But I couldn't stay inside Talbot's walls and mend my broken body and mind forever. I was being eased out. My weekend trips to my parents' place had been testing enough, and more daunting outings were looming.

My first 'day out' without my parents and the Talbot staff was with ten of my closest girlfriends to Miss Marple's restaurant in Olinda, a 40-minute trip in a friend's low yellow sportscar. I was emotionally stressed before the outing even began. The thought of leaving the Talbot grounds and entering a place where medical assistance was unavailable triggered huge anxiety. Of course I was excited at the return of my social life and the opportunity to prove to my friends that I had made gains, but deep down I feared how they would cope with caring for me outside the rehab centre. And indeed the trip did not go to plan.

Not only did my wheelchair not fit in the car, the transfers in and out of the vehicle were awkward and uncomfortable. My friends were well meaning but lacked the professional touch of the carers I was used to. Another issue that I hadn't predicted was the difficulty of trying to hear my friends speak over the car radio and café buzz.

The emotional impact of that outing outlasted the physical toll. I was grateful that my friends were prepared to include me but I was so embarrassed on their behalf. They'd gone out of their way and I felt I'd only made them feel totally helpless. By the end of the outing, each one of the deficits I had tried so hard to conceal had boldly exhibited itself. I collapsed onto my bed, slurring my thanks in an ataxic monotonous manner. For days after, my ears were ringing from the chatter and my neck ached from sitting in a low-backed chair.

These weekend outings tested me sorely, but a bigger challenge was fast approaching. Towards the end of my stay at Talbot, a post-operative scan and consultation with my surgeon was arranged in Sydney. This was an important milestone in my recovery. After several months the swelling was expected to have resolved and the level of brain damage could be determined. I was anxious. *Had my recovery-time ended? Was this it? Surely the scan would show that my brain was still floating in fluid and needed more time to settle.* Not only was I terrified about leaving the premises but I also had to fly interstate again, returning to the exact spot where I'd had my stroke.

If a café outing had seemed hard, dealing with airports and cabs took me way outside my comfort zone and made me realise I was far from healed emotionally. Worst of all, though, the scan results revealed what I had dreaded. The swelling around my brain had resolved, which meant I was stuck with the deficits I had. I was devastated. Nothing was going to get better by itself. Everything from now on was up to me.

I felt as though I needed more time if I was going to have the strength to face the future positively. My Talbot team, though, had a different agenda. They believed I had made all the gains I could under their care, and were already planning for my inevitable discharge into the community, where I would be 'handballed' to another lot of therapists. I began a series of discharge appraisals to reassess my level of disability for this new team. Having discharged patients in my past life, I knew that this was a necessary process to free up beds and also eventually for the patient's benefit. But I secretly hoped that it might be different for me. *Perhaps, being a past therapist, I could stay within the safety of Talbot's walls.*

Many of my deficits, like my eye problems and ongoing nerve pain, were now out of my teams' knowledge areas and likely to be impacting my rehabilitation, so referrals were made to seek the expertise of specialists, like pain doctors and ophthalmologists. The fact that my own neuro-specific medical team didn't know the answers was terrifying. I felt thrown into the too-hard basket. I was also hugely frustrated that beneficial treatments like the ESTIM machine (an electrical device targeting certain muscle groups), recommended to treat my facial palsy, was not used in Victoria. I therefore would have to arrange my own treatment interstate. *(Were there other treatments out there that I was missing out on?)*

The medical professionals' uncertainty about my prognosis and future intervention only fed my fear. I felt that my therapy was being left in my own incompetent hands. I became anxious about trying new things, afraid that rather than improving I'd only trigger other symptoms. My concern about the side effects of new pain medications, the chance of developing epilepsy after my craniotomy, the possibility of falling or choking, became forefront in my mind. I began to doubt all recommendations.

My anxiety was only heightened when I was referred to psych for a standard discharge tool, a neuropsychological assessment. This would ascertain my cognitive state for 'life after'. *Surely*

I didn't need yet another assessment when I had been declared cognitively unscathed by my stroke. But it was a compulsory measure that I had to undertake. There were so many patients, both on the ward and whom I'd seen in the past, who seemed to lack insight into their new persona. They seemed unaware that they had short-term memory loss, for example. I needed to be tested, but the prospect of exposing more deficits was frightening. I began to question my own mind and ability, wondering, *Do I really still have the same personality?*

In the middle of all these anxieties I surprised myself with how well I could cope 'outside'. Before my stroke, a friend had asked me to deliver a reading at her wedding. I now doubted whether I could even do this and if she still wanted me to because when she asked me I was not looking like this. But this overwhelming feeling of inadequacy was short-lived. My team learnt of my immense fear about the upcoming event and set out to ensure that I felt confident to deliver the reading. My speech therapist worked with me on articulating the script, breaking the words down into syllables and marking the verses with places to breathe. At the same time, the physio focused on my balance and endurance while standing and talking. The bride-to-be had the words written in the congregation's orders of service to help people decipher my muffled voice and my twin sister practised holding me up. I was a swaying flagpole. This support was amazing and, although feeling so vulnerable, I felt propped up by my entire team (from therapist to family) to practise.

Soon enough my discharge destination was set and my parents' home was assessed by my OT. *This isn't needed*, I thought. *I am an OT and know what I need*. I was against any permanent modifications she recommended. Not only would it unnecessarily damage their home, it would also imply that I wasn't going to improve and was destined to live with them forever.

But things had to be put in place and soon enough their home was modified. My family were given a date to take on full responsibility for their partially fixed 'Old Em'. As my family members had been very involved in my care at Talbot and were familiar now with my new needs, it was assumed that they'd manage easily to care for me in the next phase. But aside from old *What Is a Stroke?* pamphlets I'd collected from the dusty stack in the therapy zone, they were given very little education or guidance on where to next. I can't fathom how other patients with no family support would cope.

The social worker organised a disability pension, a parking permit and once again forms were signed on my behalf. The OT took me out to 'real' cafés and recommendations for community services were made. A few disciplines even arranged joint sessions to include my current and future therapists and team, including my family members. This made the transition into the next phase less daunting for all of us and I felt that my team were all on the same page.

My eventual exit from Talbot was not how I'd imagined it. I had pictured myself running out of the place, with arms full of the personal items that had decorated my room. In my mind, my disability would either evaporate or stay within the Talbot walls. Instead my dad pushed me out through the doors in a wheelchair, with my belongings stacked on my knees. My disability and I were still very much an item.

Chapter 25
A Dependent, Disabled Baby Returns Home

The transition from rehabilitation into the community was a rude shock. I was moving back to live with my parents. Mum and Dad are both unbelievable people, but watching *Gardening Australia* on a Saturday night was not what I'd envisaged I'd be doing at the age of 25. In my mind, I wanted to continue enjoying the social weekends I'd always had and go out with friends.

When I'd been home on weekend leave from the centre, the house had always been packed with visitors. Everyone had dropped their plans and fussed around me, and I had been the focus of my parents' unwavering attention. Now I was suddenly aware that I was just one of their four children. Everyone's world no longer revolved around me. The number of visitors dwindled. My twin sister booked a one-way ticket to Europe. Although I wanted Bec to stick around, I knew with her go-getting nature she needed to get on with her own life.

Distractions from the reality of my new life were becoming scarce, especially during the week's normal working hours. Five days a week I went to physio and the OT at Talbot and the speech therapist would visit regularly. But this regime as an outpatient wasn't enough for me. I was determined to fix myself. After all, I was a health professional and surely knew what had to be done. I bought an exercise bike, weights, pool noodles, a balance board, some TheraBands and a treadmill, and began my own program. I would spend hours walking with my frame up and down my parents' hallway, leaving track marks on the carpet and dents in the walls from my zig-zag gait.

Being stuck at home and the routine of Dad driving me to daily outpatient therapy really began to get to me. There were days when I'd had enough. I longed to slam a door, swear with frustration, hop in my car and burn off to a coffee shop. But my physical limitations meant that the people I was frustrated with and wanted to escape from were the ones I had to ask to take me out for a break. I must have driven my parents crazy, but they stayed eternally tolerant, happily cutting short a phone conversation to help me go to the bathroom, or pausing their favourite television programs to help me carry my frame down the front veranda stairs.

I felt useless. In the past I would have contributed, helped around the house, cooked and cleaned. Now I needed them for every move I made. I couldn't communicate my needs easily because my words were slurred and still hard to understand. Still to this day my 'phone' is mistaken for 'frame'! How I wish when they bring me my mobile it could get me to the bathroom. Apart from my difficulty pronouncing words, I had hardly any control over how my voice sounded. Either I could barely be heard or what I was trying to say came out sounding like an angry shout. I was a difficult, dependent, disabled baby.

Running had once been my physical and emotional outlet. Now I needed something to replace the essential time-out it had given me. Relearning to swim became my next focus so I began lessons at the local pool. My family drove me and reluctantly let me enter the water, watching anxiously from the sidelines. It was demeaning – blowing bubbles, coordinating my limbs in a kicking motion, and trying to swim in a straight line.

I would try to inconspicuously slide into the water but I stood out. Fellow swimmers stared and veered away from me as I struggled to stand upright in the water. I soon learnt that in order to safely practise my many exercises, like turning in a circle or marching on the spot, I needed to be away from 'bombing' swimmers or giant floating mats full of screaming kids.

It was the beginning of entering the outside world and realising how differently people saw me. One day I was water-walking to and fro in the 'aqua-play' lane and sensed dagger stares from a middle-aged lady. She walked over, crouched down at the pool's edge, and beckoned me over, curling her index finger and reeling me in like a fish. "You don't swim and drink, Girl!" she whispered disapprovingly, then stood up and walked away shaking her head. She thought I was drunk … I could explain … But she was gone.

During the week, in between my rehab appointments, Mum and I hit the shops. Shopping became my new day job, with my mum as my designated driver and shopping partner. Not wanting to be associated with the word disabled, I was deeply embarrassed by her search for a disabled car spot. I'd rather have walked.

Previously a shopaholic, I quickly learnt that I no longer loved this activity. Not only did my fellow shoppers have more time to stare at me, but entering glassware shops or places where the aisles were too cluttered or narrow was a nightmare. Shopkeepers either fussed around moving breakables or just stood back and watched anxiously, hoping that their set-up would deter my entrance.

Then there were the clothes shops that I had once loved. Trying on clothes now meant lying on the cold floor of the change rooms, arms held high, with my mum 'hula hooping' the garment over my head. After struggling to put on the item, I'd check out the spinning, double image of my reflection. Far from liking what I saw, I'd often just buy the item to save energy. Instead of giving me her normal motherly advice of, "It's a bit revealing" or "It won't wash well," Mum would just say, "It looks great on you, Em!" I guess anything was better than tracksuits and PJs. Determined to prove that I would soon return to my old lifestyle, I often bought completely unsuitable work attire, skirts and shirts that needed ironing or required lots of buttoning.

Indoor shopping centres were a place where Mum and I were rudely confronted with the reality of life outside my comfort zone. It was great to practise my balancing, walking up and down the aisles with a supermarket trolley, and trialling using my distorted speech with strangers, but there were many obstacles: lifts not working, slippery floors, steep ramps, knocking items off shelves and copping glares or inappropriate comments from strangers, were just a few.

It was also the beginning of seeing how we would both react to these obstacles. I became acutely aware of how these incidents impacted my mum. I remember the first time a lady raced to grab a seat that I was about to claim at a crowded Gloria Jean's café…

"Sorry, my daughter was about to sit on that seat, do you mind if I take it?" Mum explained, anticipating the lady's positive response.

To Mum's horror, the woman barked firmly, "No, this seat's taken. Sorry."

Mum looked perplexed, dumbfounded. I could see her mind searching for a comeback. Her hands clutched onto the back of the chair. *She isn't going to let this go*, I thought. Fearing a scene, when I already stood out in every situation, I stopped her, pointed to the counter stools and staggered over, hoping that she'd follow.

"Don't worry, Ma," I said calmly, although I was just as bewildered at the lady's response.

"I can't believe it, Em. The nerve!" Mum huffed, pushing my stool in and shaking her head in the wrongdoer's direction.

"Ma, it's a waste of energy, just enjoy lunch." Seeing how angry and protective Mum was really upset me.

That night I wrote in my diary:

A stranger took my seat at a café. Mum's brown hair turned greyish with horror, like a mood ring. I'll try harder to seem not bothered by strangers' inappropriate actions and comments. It upsets Mum too much.

The longer I spent living back at home, the more I became aware of the huge sacrifice my parents had to make to their lifestyle to accommodate me. It was comforting that they were so willing to do this, but also terrifying. Dad had stopped work, they'd modified their home, and their social routine had completely changed. If one went out, the other stayed home to 'babysit' me.

It was reassuring to see Mum occasionally gardening and seeing her many friends, but increasingly I feared they were stopping doing what they enjoyed and isolating themselves. I felt responsible. It was hard to step out of the little self-focused bubble I existed within, but I tried to continue to show that I appreciated them. I even nominated Dad for 'Father of the Year Award' and he deservingly won! When we collected the award we both had to tolerate the embarrassment of being surrounded by seven-year-old kids who'd also nominated their dads.

When Dad said that he had booked a trip to Antarctica, I was so excited that he was going to do something that he enjoyed, outside 'Em's world'. I was torn between wanting him to have his life back and dreading him moving on without me. It was as if he was choosing to go forward and join every other person in this fast-paced world and might never come back. Oddly, I was just as emotionally confused when he returned.

DIARY EXCERPT 25TH FEBRUARY 2007

Dad returns from his Antarctica trip today. I can envisage him emerging from the plane terminal. In my mind, he'll stop and take a long deep breath to soak up every last bit of oxygen, preparing to return to his 'caring' role. He'll bend down, get a firm grip on his luggage and inwardly say, "Here we go." I hate that his holiday has ended. I hate that when he sees me I'll have made no gains. My only gain will be yet another eye ulcer!

Desperate for my own holiday, in the first year of my recovery I often stayed with my older sister Kate and her husband Doug in New South Wales. I felt so accepted there and flourished on their empathy. I was envious of their happy, secure marriage but so grateful that they were prepared to include me in their lifestyle. Throughout her first pregnancy, Kate and I played Scrabble, and enjoyed pedicures and coffees together. It was the time-out I needed. In fact, her first baby became my motivation to try everything I could do to speed up my recovery. My niece or nephew was not going to have a disabled auntie or see me walk with a frame.

During those visits Doug, a physiotherapist, would spend hours manipulating my limbs or giving me exercises, attempting to dim my raging pain. He also stoked my motivation and casually planted seeds of coping strategies, recommending self-help books and programs. Often he listened to my many frustrations while taking me to lookouts, beach walks or on drives. My visits there gave me a break from my rehabilitation and were exactly what I needed. I'm sure they also gave my parents respite from their caring roles.

There were times, too, when I needed respite from Mum and Dad, and my friends rescued me and took me out. I'd once loved large groups and, as an extrovert, was always a lively player in any discussion. Now I was on the sidelines watching, grieving that I could no longer participate like I had. If I mustered up the courage to add to a conversation, trying to cut into the others' loud chatter was impossible. I must've looked like a fish, opening and shutting my mouth but saying nothing. Often, one person would notice my unsuccessful attempt and say, "Em has something to say." Then all eyes would be on me, the room would go silent, but not only had the topic passed but under pressure my words came out all wrong in an awful slur.

I somehow assumed my close friends would understand all the things that were wrong with me, but how could I have expected this of them? None of them had seen my medical records, and I hadn't bothered to explain many of my deficits to them because I didn't want more of their pity. When we went out, it couldn't be to a loud venue, or one with stairs. We had to get a parking spot nearby because my walking was slow and difficult. I was painfully conscious of hindering them and, I felt, negatively tainting the occasion. *I was a burden.*

My friends were caring and looked after me so well but neither they nor or I really took into account my physical limitations. I was determined to fit back into a normal life and reciprocate their efforts, but my body constantly let me down …

One day they organised an amazing picnic to celebrate Christmas. There we all were, sprawled on the grass enjoying the delicious food they'd brought. After a short time I realised I needed to go to the toilet. I was busting. "Don't make a fuss," I told myself, hating being reliant on them. I quietly asked for help. But by the time my friends had understood the urgency and begun looking for a non-existent loo it was too late. I had wet myself.

Not only was it deeply embarrassing, I also felt I had let them down. None of us had factored in my disability needs in choosing the venue. Back then, we were all on a steep learning curve and I didn't even know my own needs to be able to brief them.

Over that period I really missed Bec, who was still travelling overseas. Part of me had foolishly assumed that she would stay by my side until I was well enough to escape with her. I would jealously hear about her travels. Even though she continually sent letters, photos and called, it was hard to accept that she'd moved on. When she returned from her trip, she went back to her busy lifestyle, doing all the things I had planned to do. She began dating a great guy, Paul, who had never met me prior to my stroke. 'Meeting the parents' is always daunting, but having to meet a disabled sister as well, I'm sure was terrifying. *Would it change his feelings about Bec?* I hated contemplating that I might impact her path more than I had already.

But thankfully that didn't happen. Bec and Paul decided to work abroad and on Boxing Day, 2006, while in France, she unexpectedly called me with the news that Paul had proposed. She was going to get married in 2008. Despite feeling shock at her announcement, I was so excited for her. Paul had been wonderful for Bec and was an amazingly calming, observant and patient guy, full of drive and integrity. He would be a thoughtful and caring brother-in-law for me and if our twin-ness was to be divided by anyone, he was the perfect choice.

By now Kate had given birth to a baby girl, my gorgeous niece Lucy. With the excitement of that and Bec's engagement, the winds of change were blowing around me, but I felt my life was stationary, going backwards even. There I was, still living at home as a disabled adult child. It was sorely testing all of us. I'd always had a great relationship with my family and friends but having them now as my carers was changing the dynamics of our lives.

Chapter 26
The New Me Steps Out into the World

After over six months living at my parents' home, I was feeling stuck and too reliant on others to care for me. *I just wanted to get on with life.* Experiences like shopping with Mum had shown me that people saw me very differently now. In my parents' homey environment I had begun to get used to my own deficits, but once outside that familiar front door, everything changed. There were so many obstacles, I could see why many people would give up in this phase. The world doesn't seem to want you back in this form, and those who love and accept you don't want to let you go out and experience failure.

But a return-to-work appointment in the city was the perfect opportunity to go beyond home and shopping centres and tackle public transport with my new frame.

Catching a train will be so easy. Once I could have run this route blind-folded, I think. Declaring my intentions to my parents, however, signals a major battle.

"You'll break a leg … this time you'll be doing rehab alone." And later "If you must do it, do it with your mother." Even with

Mum accompanying me, they thought I was setting myself up for failure. *My parents are saying catching a train is too dangerous. Imagine what they'll be like when I start driving again!*

Getting ready is the first step in preparing to enter the danger zone. It's no fashion parade going out with a disability. Eye ointment replaces eyeliner; lipstick only magnifies the deep crevices in my sore, wonky lips. My fashionable wardrobe is now useless.

Mum parks the car while I tackle the seemingly endless ramps leading to the platform. First the declines, I breathe. I had once run downhill, arms out like the wings of a plane and eyes closed. Now, I try to test out my former running coach's theory that shifting your weight backwards helps. *Disastrous!* Instead, I end up squatting to prevent somersaulting down. All I can see and hear around me are feet. Heels, sneakers, heels. Heels. All walking with ease. Two out of the 50 people that pass ask if I need help. To the others I am invisible or they're just too busy rushing to make the train, Vegemite toast or mobile in hand.

We are getting the 8.19am train. Waiting on the platform, I must look as if I'm starting a race, my frame positioned at the very edge of the yellow line. The doors open but before I've even managed to cross the line the 'beep beep beep' sound signals that the doors are about to shut. Mum is in the carriage, but my frame and I are still on the platform.

"JUMP ON, EM!" shouts Mum, terrified at the prospect of her daughter falling down the big black space in between the train and platform. They hadn't covered jumping in rehab, but looking at Mum's face I know I have to get across that abyss somehow.

I monkey-bar on, my knuckles white from strangling the rail inside the carriage door, my eyes struggling to adjust to the light change. Mum and I have decided to travel separately so I can try to be independent. But I can sense her watching me as she hovers anxiously at the other end of the carriage. *I have to appear calm for her sake.* But before I can find a seat, the carriage lurches forward and I plummet sideways into the lap of a stranger.

After recovering from that embarrassment, I settle into my new 'disabled' seat and I watch the world spin by. As a kid, I'd always been amazed at how your eyes flick back and forth trying to capture every passing image – graffiti, people, traffic lights, trees, all blurred. In a speeding train my nystagmus (flickering of the eyes) feels normal. Since my operation, my eyes have raced. They are the only body parts that move quickly. Two images, both racing.

A schoolgirl sits opposite me reading *To Kill a Mocking Bird*, a novel I had read and studied. She's a nerd, I think to myself. The extended academic strip on the left pocket of her blazer, her long, ironed dress and braided hair are proof. Finding flaws in others is somehow gratifying. Their imperfections help take the focus off mine.

A small child tugs her mother's dress demandingly. Her eyes seem super-glued to me, as if I might swallow her if she loses track of me. "Mummy, why's that girl got that thing?" She points directly at my frame. Her mum, embarrassed, grabs her out-stretched hand, saying, "She needs it to walk, Sweetie. Now don't stare."

I hate that kids say out loud what adults think!

An elderly woman standing on the unstable train floor, clearly showing off her good balance, sees me reaching for my bag at my feet and says, "Do you want help, Dear?" Stubborn and knowing that the help I need is endless, I reply, "No thanks."

A bearded man approaches me and says loudly, "What's wrong with you?" and then pointing at me, "You got MS?"

Shocked by his bluntness all I say is, "No," secretly hoping that my concise reply will imply that I don't want to reveal my medical status to a stranger, let alone the entire carriage. Perhaps my frozen facial paralysis misleads him, because he keeps on guessing. He plonks down beside me. "It's muscular dystrophy isn't it?" And then even louder and slower, "Ummmmmmmm, I know. It's cerebral palsy!" He is almost excited by his diagnosis.

Knowing that he will continue quizzing me with a hospital full of diagnoses I say, "I had a stroke." *There … I'd said it. Just go away.*

The train stops suddenly and a white cane zigzags on board, followed by a blind man. I immediately turn away, knowing that others will stare. But then his self-assured manner prompts me to turn back. *How could he be blind but look as though he is walking on red carpet? How are his physical limitations riding with him but not directing his route?* I realise that unlike him I still see myself as a victim. His attitude helps me become aware of the power of choice. I decide to try on my survivor suit. Getting off the train is now my focus.

I make it out of the train but crossing Flinders Street is a ten-minute ordeal for me and Mum. "Let's go." I snap. She pulls me back. *She stresses me out.* One impatient commuter beeps his horn at me as we take the plunge. Mum's glare silences any future honks. I convince myself that if she hadn't been with me it would've been a breeze.

Having arrived in the big city, Mum reluctantly leaves. I'm independent at last, alone with my frame. My appointment is 55 minutes away, just enough time for a coffee.

I enter the nearest café trying to make my disability less conspicuous. My turtle pace forces the impatient caffeine-deprived queue to trail outside the door. I wait my turn to be served, but I'm invisible. They seem to serve everyone but me. I practise saying my order inside my head while I simultaneously try and get my balance. "One skim cappuccino with a straw please." *Perfect, my therapist would be impressed*, I think, chuffed.

It's my turn. "A cap … with str …"

It comes out all wrong and before I've even finished my order the waitress hastily says, "That'll be $3.30." And then, "Who's next?"

I try again. "Could I have a straw with my coffee?"

Puzzled by my query she replies, "Sorry Ma'am, um, strawberries aren't in season yet," and then goes on serving. "Next!"

A stranger in the queue behind me interrupts, "No. She wants a straw."

"Oh … sure." the waitress says, bewildered at my request.

Only 30 minutes left before my appointment. The crammed café forces me to perch on a stool next to a smelly man. He croaks, "Mate, I'm so tired. You've no idea."

In terms of tiredness, at this point I feel 'the queen of fatigue', but I have to remind myself that it's all relative. I sip my coffee through my long-fought-for straw, slurping the last bit of fluid. I need it.

I glance at my mobile. It's 10.45. I have one new text: "EMMA, APPOINTMENT CANCELLED. MELANIE SICK. RING TO REBOOK."

My therapist is away sick. My appointment is cancelled. My double vision confirms my disbelief. What a waste! I still have to cross the road and catch the train home. I can't waste my energy getting upset. *Survivors don't cry*, I think, holding my tears back.

~

That day was a brutal beginning, not a taste but a gutful of society's misconceptions about disability. As a therapist I had listened to patients' stories of their misadventures in the outside world. Now I was living them.

I now inhabited two worlds. The outside world I had just ventured into seemed to treat me as invisible or a nuisance. In the other protected world of those who empathised with my condition, I was often patronised. Proving to these people that although I was physically impacted I still remained cognitively unscathed, became one of my biggest challenges.

Typically they would bend down to me, put their hand on my knee sympathetically and slowly and loudly say, "My Name is Penny. Do you understanD me?" With every syllable I would cringe. If I could've physically kicked them, pinned them to the ground and said, *"No. Do you understand me?"* I would've. Afterwards, I'd often relay the conversation to my sister or friends and we'd laugh. Humour was medicine of a sort, but the laughter was short-lived and moments like this scorched my confidence like a hot poker and were tattooed on me for life.

Just as bad as the long slow talkers were those who ignored me and seemed to direct every question to whoever was with me. "Does she want her hair blow dried?" they would enquire, without even looking in my direction. My friends would deliberately refuse to give the stranger eye contact. Instead, they would look at me, saying, "Ask Em, she'll tell you."

Then there were the ones who asked me a question but wouldn't wait for the time it took me to get my halting answer out. "Would you like coffee or tea, Lovey?"

I'd be dying for a nice coffee and would happily invest energy in my reply, "Coffee, please."

But it was obvious they didn't listen to my response when they put a cup of tea on the table in front of me, saying, "Here's your cuppa, Sweetie."

Although their words were well meaning, in my vulnerable state I perceived their behaviour as deliberate and destructive. Negative thoughts viciously cycled in my mind and damaged my self-esteem even further. I was still having weekly outpatient therapy at Talbot, so at least I was able to share these experiences with my therapy team. My speech therapist helped me practise short and concise responses to prove to strangers that I was cognitively OK, and the psychologist allowed me to vent, and develop strategies to help me better cope with life outside. For example, when I bumped into a person from my past in the street, I learnt to quickly address them by name or bring up some earlier shared incident to prove my memory was still fine. On other occasions we looked at my feelings and how I could control my reaction to the inappropriate words and actions of strangers. These therapy sessions became a needed break and an opportunity to stop trying to keep pace and allow my emotions to catch up. There I could reflect on how I was surviving in life outside, and feel safe to express both my good and bad experiences. I felt heard, accepted and tolerated. Continuing writing in a journal was another ongoing means of coping. This was the beginning of developing the habits that were vital to staying well balanced in the future.

Chapter 27
Taking My Disability on Holiday

A break from my rehabilitation seemed exactly what I needed at this stage, a chance to figure out my next move. But my first 'holiday' with my mum, a friend and her mum was a huge shock for us all. It was definitely *not* the mother and daughter trip I'd envisaged. Not only did I need help to drag my unwanted disability around, I was unable to do the activities I'd previously done, like swim and sunbake. Plus it felt wrong to be travelling with my mum after years of holidaying with boyfriends and friends.

I was no longer a beach babe. Now I needed to fiercely grasp my frame, with no hands free to adjust my bathers when I had a wedgy. It didn't help that the weather was shocking and our hotel was evacuated on two occasions due to a dysfunctional fire alarm. Unable to quickly or safely exit, I had to rely on a stranger to help. He threw my vulnerable, pyjama-clad body over his shoulder like a sack of potatoes and ran!

Holidaying with my disability encroached on all areas of my life. Over those six days I tried to keep up and act like the Old Em, but my stubborn attempts to appear normal began to taint the holiday and the others' enjoyment of it. Fed up with trudging through muddy water on my walking frame, I succumbed to using a wheelchair. *Frame or wheelchair? What a choice. My companions had to either wait for me or push me.*

I was there to relax and recuperate but it was difficult to rest, knowing how much work was ahead of me. Taking a break meant I had time to process all that had happened to me. I craved distraction, but the more I was out of my familiar environment the more I became aware of what I could no longer do. It was the beginning of the realisation that things became harder, not easier, on holidays.

I loved escaping my rehab life, but dragging my disability to each holiday destination was not part of the plan. My parents' beach house in Anglesea was a regular getaway where I'd discover new deficits and begin testing how I'd holiday with others…

I'm sitting in a comfy brown recliner overlooking the ocean. This spot is sheltered from the pesky March flies I can no longer swat, away from the hot sand that I can't run over, and the itchy heat that triggers my pain. *Here I am safe. Safe, but distant. Detached. I feel smothered by dependency.*

Mum's earlier suggestion that, "It would be good for you to go for a short walk" is unthinkable. I want to go on a long walk now! The truth is, I want to go on a long, hilly run. I want to scream, "What'd be *good* for me is if my double vision, poor balance and speech impediment resolved!"

It's impossible to rest when I have so far to go to return to my pre-stroke life. I force myself to contemplate the consequences of not moving. Nerve pain plus! *I need to walk.* I heave my body up and stagger to the top of the staircase and abruptly stop. I am stuck here until my frame can be lifted down the stairs. *A baby bird that can't fly.*

Mum and Dad's eyes track my steps.

"Where are you off to, Em?" Mum asks, sitting bolt upright.

"Just going for a walk to the beach," I reply, looking straight ahead so they won't see my tears.

"Really, Em, that's a long way. Dad will drive you."

"Ma, I want to walk."

"David, can you drive Em to the beach?"

"Ma, I want to walk!"

"Oh OK. Want me to come, Em?"

"No," I say.

"I'll just turn the oven off so the scones don't burn and help you down the stairs."

Her assumption that I'll need her assistance makes depending on her that much easier. I'm sick of asking for help to complete every task, so I wait for the help that I don't want. I focus on standing upright and keeping my tears of frustration at bay.

Mum lifts my frame down the stairs, puts on my shoes, helps me zip my jacket and grabs my phone that I've left upstairs. I thank her in my head and then leave her reluctantly on the nature strip. She hugs her ribs anxiously to stop herself reaching out to adjust my jacket collar or to move the twig from my frame's path. "Are you sure you don't want me to come … I've got nothing else to do," she calls behind me.

"Ma!" I keep walking.

"OK, if you're sure … See you at the beach, Honey. Dad and I will have the car there waiting for you."

So I make my way to the beach. Rather than taking the uneven sandy scenic path that I used to run on, I take the safer road route. *Loose pebbles are more of a hazard than an oncoming car nowadays.* I sense Mum's distant presence but am not game to look back. Any slight change in my direction will throw me off-balance, and force Mum to run and rescue my collapsed body. The prospect of her hugging me tightly saying, "I thought this would happen, Darling," fuels my determination to climb the ten metres up the hill without panting, stooping or tipping. As the hill becomes steeper I muster up more speed, picking up momentum so I don't roll backwards. When I turn the corner and am out of Mum's sight I allow myself to stop and let out a big long shaky sigh.

~

On that holiday I felt desperate. That day as I walked away from my parents I was so tempted to collapse into the gutter and just curl up with the rest of the rubble and howl. *If a car hits me, I'll secretly be glad. It's a good excuse for not finishing this walk.* Pretending that I didn't want to stay in front of the warm fire, or get a hug, was tough. I was secretly grateful that Mum tried to wrap me in cotton wool. Her motherly ways frustrated me, but the fact that she flagged issues out loud that I already feared, meant that I felt less alone. I could let another do the worrying for a bit. Knowing that the safety net was there, I was more willing to step beyond my comfort zone.

~

An hour later my parents are waiting in the beach car park. "How was it, Em?" Dad enquires.

"Easy," I lie, adopting a semi-relaxed stance. I want to practise my walking alone. They reluctantly leave me on the sand.

A guy runs by – the beach run I long for. *This is too hard.* I give up practising my sand walk, fall in a heap and crawl only metres from where I'd been left. Sitting there, I remember the many beach runs and sand-dune sprints I've done – here, Zanzibar, Port Douglas … *I want to run over and dive fully clothed into the ocean. Fully clothed, not because I need help undressing but because I so miss the spontaneity of my old life.*

My left foot is now blue and cold. Corpse like. I could walk on hot bricks with my left foot and not flinch. A new party trick. Fire twirling and ice sculptures are dated, I think bitterly. One thing I know is that I can't run barefoot to the ocean for a quick dip anymore. My brain now misinterprets the "Em, your feet are burning" signal and delays it. Then a few minutes later my body endures a pain response that lasts about eight hours.

My parents soon return to see the bum tracks behind me, like a snail. It's obvious I just crawled. *No footprints as planned.* I'm relieved to see them, but don't show it. I'm too exhausted to pretend I don't need their help. I let them heave me up, shake the sand off my legs and put me in the car.

When I was a teenager, going away with my parents was embarrassing. Now the roles were probably reversed. Although I was well aware that it was their holiday too, I didn't allow myself to exit my self-indulgent bubble to see the impact that my behaviour was having on them. It really was no holiday for any of us.

CHAPTER 28
Dependent Independence!

After 12 long months of living with my parents, I decided to begin looking to live independently. Although I definitely felt welcome to stay with Mum and Dad, I longed for my own space. Every Saturday, Dad and I spent time circling ads for potential units and then viewing one or two of them. It was impossible to do more than that in one day because of my turtle pace. Plus, many were automatically excluded. I needed a place without stairs, with carpet, wide doorframes, and close to public transport and my parents.

"That was good, Em. What do you think?" Dad would say after the inspection.

"The carpet's a bit of a weird colour," I'd reply, having only concentrated on the floor in front of me because of my visual and mobility problems.

Basically I was reliant on Dad's opinion. Navigating each property was terrifying. I was worried about people's judgemental stares, about scraping the walls with my frame or leaving tyre marks on the freshly vacuumed carpet.

I guess Dad and I had a mutual purpose in our search. I wanted to get out and I'm sure he wanted to live again without kids. At auctions Dad bid for me and I waited in the car with a mobile phone to track whether I'd been sold my independence ticket. Eventually I bought a unit only a few suburbs away from my parents' home.

The chance to be independent was so exciting, but as I looked around my new, empty home I felt overwhelmed and alone. *Everything is trapped in big boxes that I rely on others to empty. I know where I want things put but can't move to put them there.* It was the beginning of a dark and growing feeling of dependent independence that I still lug around today.

My unit was a sanctuary, a place to sit in my chair in silence, recovering from the fast-paced life outside. But at first I found the many nights alone quite difficult. Even my Saturday nights watching TV documentaries with my parents had been at least a diversion, with the bonus of an amazing home-cooked meal. On my own it was so quiet and didn't seem worth cooking for one. Although I had a dog, Morgan, the golden retriever, he didn't come with me because he didn't fit in my small courtyard. That was my excuse, anyway. Really I knew I couldn't care for him and my parents soon gave him to another family. I felt I'd failed as an owner. Determined to prove to others and myself that I could care for another, I began researching 'cat-like dogs' and found a golden cavoodle that I named Gilbert. Not being able to care for him in the normal way was initially quite confronting. *Was I depriving him of his puppyhood?* Friends reassured me, "He knows no different, Em."

It was an odd kind of independence. I reluctantly accepted that I still needed help to care for Gilbert and myself. To be eligible for any service from community organisations, though, I had to highlight in each assessment what I could no longer

Lyn Gee cradling her newborn baby girl twins on the 28/7/1980.

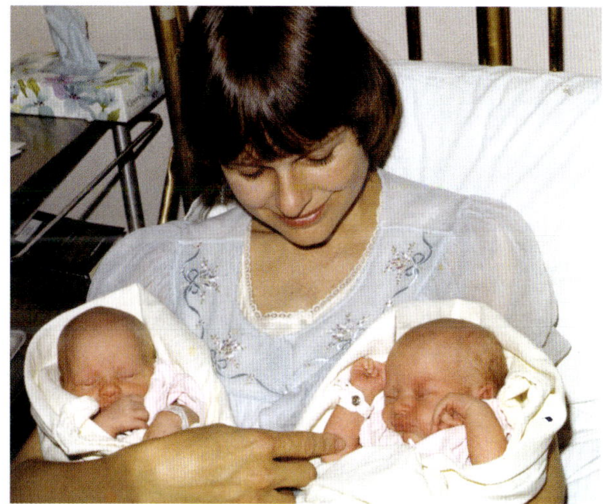

(*Right*) Em and Bec's first day of school, Melbourne 1986. / (*Below left*) Sisters and best friends three days before their lives changed forever. Em's last trip with her girlfriends to Anglesea, 2005. / (*Below right*) Em graduates with a Bachelor of Occupational Therapy, LaTrobe University 2003.

Reaching the peak of Mt Kinabalu, Malaysia at sunrise (Fi, Kiri, Em and Al). This climb in April 2005 precipitated Em's AVM bleed.

Em takes a break from her studies, caring for 70 street children in Arusha, Tanzania 2003.

(*Far left*) Em clicking her heels, Anglesea 2002. (*Left*) A tiny taste of the marathon ahead, Em completes the Melbourne half-marathon, 2004.

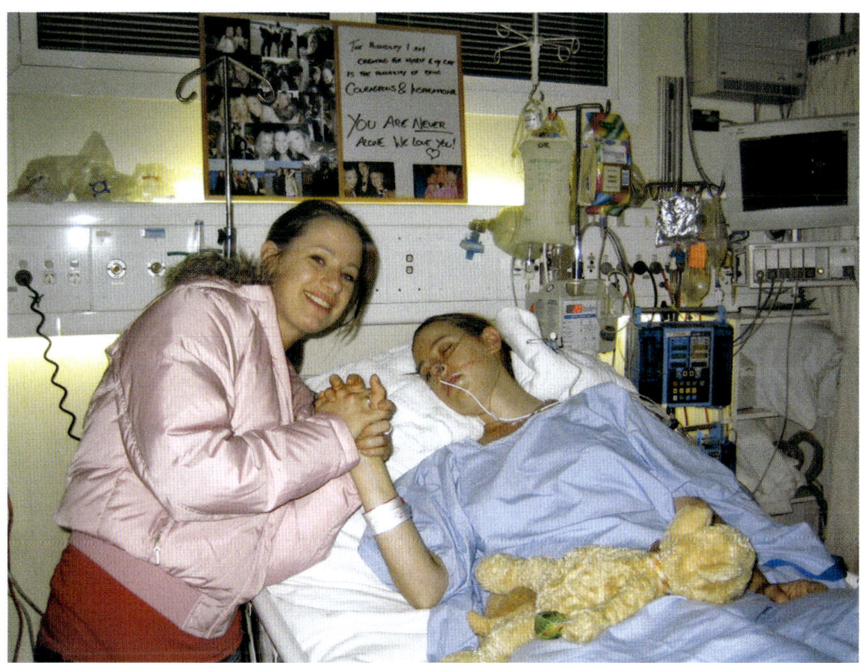

Incredible support from the beginning. Bec with Emma, still in a coma (Dalcross Hospital, NSW 2005).

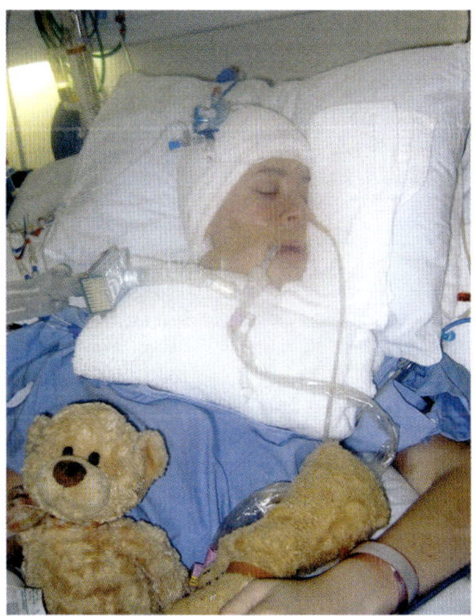

Em in a coma in Intensive Care, (Dalcross Hospital, 2005).

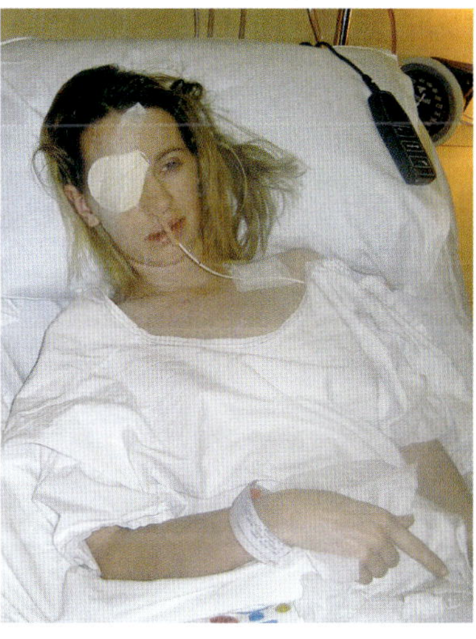

Finally out of intensive care, Em realises the huge road ahead.

Em's personalised 'communication board' devised by her sister to ensure she was able to point out her needs with her ataxic fingers and not miss! (Dalcross Hospital, 2005).

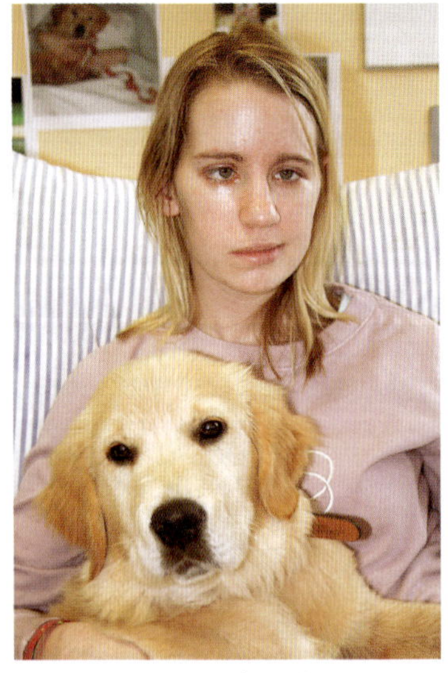

Emma resting after therapy at Talbot with her daily visitor, Morgan the dog, October 2005.

Emma's new home at Talbot, Melbourne 2005.

Em's supporters organise a fun run 'Run to Gee' Melbourne, September, 2005.

(*Right*) Em meditating. She now incorporates time in her day to stop and reflect, 2015. (*Far Right*) Em chooses to turn her world upside down in her favourite yoga pose in New Zealand, 2015. (*Bottom*) Emma relearns how to swim, floating above her pain, 2010.

Photograph © Tara Stubbs

Photograph © David Gee

Photograph © Tara Stubbs

Emma in her typical workplace, preparing for an upcoming presentation, 2015.

Emma meets The Honourable Quentin Bryce at the Beyond Blue and National Stroke Foundation DVD launch, Sydney, 2010.

Photograph © The Stroke Foundation

(*Left*) Em presents, encouraging and challenging her audiences to see things through her eyes (Melbourne, 2013). (*Below*) Em inspires many by commencing her Inspirational Speaking Business, 2012.

Photograph © Ikon Images

Em with her incredible family, Castlemaine 2014. Back row (L-R) Bec, Paul, Tom, David, Lyn, Harry, Doug. Middle row (L-R) Rach (in pink), Lucy, Holly, Kate. Front row (L-R) Em, Pete, Ellen, Olive, Jack.

Auntie Em with her brood of nieces and nephews, a major source of daily motivation, 2014. (L-R) Lucy, Harry, Em, Tom, Olive, Ellen, Holly & Jack.

Bridesmaids Kim, Em & Mel celebrate Tracey and James' wedding, Melbourne 2013.

Photograph © David Gee

Em paraglides over Queenstown, New Zealand 2015.

(*Left*) Emma enjoys time at Castlemaine with her parents, 2015. / (*Below*) Em with her siblings, 2014. (L-R Pete, Em, Bec & Kate).

do – something I preferred not to think about too much. After a number of depressing assessments I was allocated a regular carer from the council for a couple of hours a week.

The decision to let a random stranger invade my personal space was not easy. I confess that at first I was defensive, and critical of everything they did. Sometimes they'd begin tasks assuming what needed to be done. "Let's let some light in here and brighten this place up. It will cheer ya up," they might say, pulling up the shutters that I had deliberately left down to lessen the glare that hurt my now ultra-sensitive eyes. Some helped themselves to a choccy or two from an open box, flipped through a book on my bedside table or told me to do things in a different way. While I felt happy to offer them a chocolate or adopt their suggestions, the forceful way they seemed to take over my own home made me feel bitter and resentful. Watching someone else do things that I once could do for myself just rubbed in the reality of my own helplessness.

It was even tougher when they did things their way, without considering the outcome. One carer made my bed, tucking the white sheets in firmly under the mattress. She failed to realise that I didn't have the strength or the control to untuck the sheets. That night when I tried to 'post' my body between the tight sheets, I kneed myself in the face, resulting in a blood nose.

Another well-meaning carer hung my wet clothes out in the sunny courtyard to save electricity, assuming I'd just bring them in when they were dry. Once again I was made blatantly aware of the simple things I couldn't do. Not only was the step down to the courtyard a big obstacle, but taking the dry washing off, carrying it inside and folding the clothes was a huge effort.

Besides that, it was quite risky for me in my unbalanced state. Often the clothes I managed to drag in looked like they'd been folded by a two-year–old.

Now I'm able to admit that the presence of home carers in my life has been invaluable and I am so grateful for their assistance. But initially it was a frustrating time for me. Independence was within my grasp but I didn't want to admit that I needed help to get there. Even my parents' help wasn't always welcome. Their regular visits dropping off coffees and treats, or doing the gardening or dressing my eye often made me feel more disempowered. I was particularly upset if they came unannounced. And yet in the middle of the night when my pain peaked, I often called my dad for advice and just to hear his reassuring voice. On hot nights he'd uncomplainingly collect me and take me back to their air-conditioned place. My parents were remarkably patient. I must've come across like a spoilt brat. I had lost the ability to make my own decisions, but I hated that I was reliant on others to make them for me.

I was adamant about still having some control over my new home. I refused to listen to therapists' recommendations that I purchase an electric scooter to replace the rusty manual silver car that I no longer could drive, or modify my bathroom and install rails around my new home. In my state of denial I continued to stubbornly believe that putting in ugly disabled equipment was a waste of money and unnecessary when I was on my way to a 100 per cent recovery. Accepting any modifications to my home symbolised permanency and disability confinement, and suppressed any chance of hope. Those around me would assume I was no longer improving. I don't think my therapists understood my state of mind, and often took my refusals personally. Of course their suggestions were right and in fact did seed the ideas. For example, after a while of getting around in cabs and trams and depending on lifts, I decided that a funky-looking scooter would improve my independence.

Sleep, or lack of it, was an ongoing problem. My pain now peaked at night, disrupting my sleep and then my monkey mind would generate more problems. *Will I have another stroke? Will I be able to return to work? Will I ever have kids? Will I be too tired and miss my physio session tomorrow?* I'd turn my bedside light on to read, trying to distract myself from the near-exploding pain that just seemed to escalate when combined with any worries.

On those sleepless nights I would often rewind my previous day to identify the pain triggers – the culprits. *Maybe it was sitting in a hard chair in direct sun at that café? Or was it when I rolled the supermarket trolley over my numb left foot?* I would usually conclude that it was most likely a combination of all of these things, the main contributor being the weather. I was now a human barometer, supersensitive to every small temperature change.

Basically my rewired brain was interpreting all signals from my warped body as pain. I was determined to find a cure for this, constantly dragging my raging pain-racked body to new pain specialists and trialling the latest pain medications. Factoring more medical trips into my week meant I spent my days sitting in waiting rooms with Dad, rather than alone in my new place. When I couldn't sleep I would helplessly wrestle the side effects of my new tablets – nausea, spinning and, even worse, balance. In my physically unpredictable state my confidence plummeted. I felt so helpless and utterly fed up.

The elation I had felt when I moved into my new home had proved to be short-lived. My newfound independence was replaced with a feeling of helplessness, reliance and doubt. I never envisaged that well over a year after my stroke, I'd still be so heavily dependent on those around me.

Chapter 29
On the Shelf

Now that I had my own place, I naively assumed that I could finally resume my previously full social life, but I soon learnt that going out with my friends was not the same anymore. The gulf between our lives was wider than any of us wanted to admit. I could no longer relate to their endless discussions about work, paying off mortgages and boyfriend issues. Rehab was the only issue many would ask me about. I think they thought that 'normal' topics would elicit too much grief and they perhaps didn't want to remind me of what I no longer had. To make things worse, in unfamiliar surroundings my physical limitations were more noticeable. Even when I couldn't hear their conversations I mirrored others' nods and laughs to seemingly fit in for their sake, but I'd hold in my tears. *They were drifting away from me.*

Many of my friends were getting engaged, married or were pregnant, so my social life became about celebrating their milestones. Big social events were a nightmare. At times I'd be left by my walking frame in the same spot the entire night. Often I'd be standing next to no one, forcing myself to aimlessly flick through my phone as if I was busy. Or I was left sitting beside my friend's grandparent, who complained about the blaring noise, their hip pain and the youth of today. Usually, in my tired state, I would become increasingly frustrated, enviously watching my friends as they danced and drank. I left early, after speeches, my sensitive ears still ringing three days later. It didn't help that I was aware that such celebrations for me personally were unlikely.

Diary excerpt 24th february 2007

Tonight my friend came over. I said something like, "If I never marry, I'm going to buy myself a diamond ring," secretly hoping she would say something reassuring like, "Em, of course you'll marry!" But the "Good idea" response I received was hard to swallow.

If I thought going away with my family was frustrating, holidays with friends were way more difficult. Although the idea of a 'blobby' weekend away with my girlfriends sounded great, my initial efforts to appear normal and prove to my travel partners and myself that I was low-maintenance, failed dismally. Out of my familiar environment, I was only more reliant on others for help. For example, just showering was a huge task for me. My parents were mindful of this and would set up the shower for me. But this is an area that I chose not to flag to my friends, seeing it as just an added hassle. Instead, initially I tried to do it alone. With no rails or accessible seat in the shower, I opted to sit on the cold tiled floor. Also, being unable to decipher hot from cold water, it was usually safer to either not shower or have a freezing-cold shower. Eventually I'd emerge, exhausted with un-rinsed soapy hair.

"Nice long shower, Emmy?" my waiting friends in the shower queue would say chirpily. I couldn't begin to explain how awful that shower had been. I'd want to cry all the water I'd just been fighting with.

I wanted to contribute in some way but they shut down any offers to help clean up or cook. "Just rest, Em, it's all sorted". So I would just sit and watch, feeling more helpless and isolated. I became so frustrated and read their kindness as devaluing. 'Blobbing' still involved tasks that I could no longer do, like beach runs, walks and table-tennis games. My friends urged me to accompany them, but I would often choose to sit on the sidelines if I went. Or I'd stay alone at the holiday house.

Back in the city, friends were aware that going out was difficult and often came to me.

My friend is arriving in 40 minutes. I get up stiffly and make my way to the fridge to retrieve the ingredients I'd ordered from Coles online. I plan to have our dinner ready on her arrival. But by the time I've chopped half a red capsicum and a zucchini, I collapse, utterly exhausted, into a chair and reluctantly text her, *"R U OK to cook? I have all the stuff but am zapped."*

The doorbell rings and my friend enthusiastically walks into my kitchen and finishes what I barely started. I lean next to her on the Laminex bench and shuffle items around, pretending I'm helping. Being upright keeps me awake. She senses my need to help, opening the tomato-paste jar and handing me a blunt knife, saying, "Here you go, Em." She's on my right paralysed side so can't see the tears running down my left cheek. *I'm over this.* I want to be helpful but just feel in the way. *I should've ordered take-away pizzas.*

Increasingly I felt I could no longer relate to my peers. At the same time I foolishly believed I had nothing in common with other people with disabilities. When another person, elderly or disabled in some way, would point out the similarity between us I would cringe inwardly. If I did see similarities with others they were never good ones, like identifying with my grandma because we both now had to walk with a frame.

Finding any commonalities seemed to only reinforce what I'd lost. Often I would just nod agreeably, silently feeling quite different. I longed to identify with people my own age again, and to feel the comfort of twin-ness I had once felt. But all around me my friends were heading off on adventures or getting married and I was finding it harder and harder to pretend everything was the same and I could fit in.

I felt stuck in No Man's Land. I reluctantly decided to attend my local stroke support group. As a health professional, it was very confronting to admit that I needed help, to have to identify with people that would've once been my patients. My first meeting with other stroke survivors was difficult. I was a lot younger than most of them and, despite sharing many of their stroke-related issues, deep down I craved to be among my own peer group. I definitely couldn't see myself playing bowls or singing in the local choir.

It sounds harsh, but I didn't want their company to limit me. I felt that they didn't share my motivation to integrate back into the real world. Many people, pre-stroke, had married, paid off their mortgages, had kids and were now retired. They appeared content to stay put. I was not. I felt that I had to keep going. I wanted to shed my new disability as soon as I could and move on. I refused to believe that wherever I went it would shadow me.

Chapter 30
The Daily Churn of Rehab

Two years on …

Instead of waking normally to an alarm, I am once again stirred rudely by the throbbing stiffness and excruciating nerve pain that now invades and pulsates around my body. Strange signals abound, from hand numbness to sharp dagger-like pains in my head or big toe, and cramping in my left hip and calf. A year ago, one of the many pain specialists said that I had to "acknowledge these crazy symptoms but not let them stop what you do." *Easy for him to say.*

But he was right. If I worried about every sign my body gave me, I'd go insane. After trialling a pharmacy full of pills to rid me of my nerve pain, I had chosen to stop taking pain medication. The tablets didn't seem to lessen my pain and just exacerbated my other problems, like my balance. By now I knew that moving my body helped, so I would choose to start my monotonous day of rehab early.

"Today is an awesome day," I chant to myself to try to fool my brain, revving up my body before my dad arrives. He is driving me to one of my daily appointments to address, fix or prevent the worsening of my new deficits. I force a wonky smile, drop to the ground on all fours and crawl to my newly modified bathroom. After showering for six months in the disabled bathroom at my local pool, I have finally accepted my therapist's recommendations and succumbed to entirely modifying the place, levelling the shower floor and installing a shower seat and grab rails. I've even had a thermostatic valve fitted so I can't burn myself. My own warped thermostat means I can't feel the hot and cold on my left side, though I've learnt over time to double check the water temperature with my right side.

Dressing is slow as usual. I unbutton and rebutton my top three times before I get it straight, then make brekky. The effort of squeezing the runny honey bottle is too great. I resort to folding the burnt crumpets in half to save the energy of spreading.

Dad arrives on time, opening my blinds and carrying my bags. I also grab a pile of forms I need Dad's help to fill out, as I struggle nowadays to write. My right, dominant, hand shakes too much from the ataxia. Although I know what I want to write, the scribble is illegible, energy depleting and time consuming. So to save the frustration, I now type or delegate. Today I'll dictate to Dad in the waiting room.

"Dad, could you put out the rubbish? I'll just grab my shoes."

Chuffed that I'm pretty organised by 9am, I opt to leave my walking frame and I wall-walk, adding to the other fingerprints on my newly painted white walls. I reach down to grab my boring flat shoes in the bottom of my cupboard. But in my confident mindset, for a split second I stupidly forget about my poor balance. I land awkwardly headfirst in a pile of my unworn heels. *Reality hits!*

Dad hears the loud thump from the next room and finds me sprawled on the floor of my cupboard. "Are you OK, Em?" He is obviously distressed seeing me lying so still.

I don't speak. I'm unsure of what just happened.

"Are you hurt?" he asks.

"I don't know," I answer, trying to figure out which direction is up. My entire body hurts. I feel like I've been splattered into thousands of pieces. I need a minute to regroup before I can work out which bit is missing.

In Dad's car there's a coffee waiting for me. After driving in silence, he double parks outside the hospital to save me the long hike, and gets out my frame, saying, "I'll meet you in about five minutes in Suite 124, Em."

Inside I follow the speckled carpet and enter the lift. An elderly couple follow me in. My battle to manoeuvre my frame in the awkward small space is the 'lift entertainment'.

"Can I help you, Dear?" the lady says, scrunching her face up like tissue paper.

"No thanks," I say cheerfully but abruptly. I sense she wants me to explain my 'disabled look' but I don't want to be late for my appointment. Besides, I don't feel like justifying my appearance to a stranger. Instead, I look straight ahead. At level three, I thank the bald man who uses his wooden cane to hold the doors open while I slowly exit. "Poor love", the lady whispers loudly, clearly saddened by what the lift just spat out.

I slump into the extremely hard, torn vinyl chair. Dad joins me seconds later, book in hand, for the expected wait. I choose to sit in silence and not waste my eyesight reading the ancient magazines sprawled over the coffee table. I close my eyes, rest my head on the wall behind me and mentally jot down the many questions I need to ask my ophthalmologist.

~

Initially, wearing an eye patch to mask my double vision (diplopia) had been a temporary fix. But once released into my old life, I realised my distorted view of the world was not going to resolve quickly. Although I did daily eye-tracking exercises for months after my stroke, I still saw double and my left eye continued to flicker constantly because of the nystagmus. I also had no nerve supply to my right eye, so had difficulty closing my right eyelid, no sensation and no longer produced tears. When my eyes became too tired, I often resorted to wearing my pirate patch at home.

Forty-five minutes later the ophthalmologist quickly assesses my vision and concludes that my cornea is showing signs of irritation. He gives me more exercises to do, a pile of prescriptions to fill, and instructs me to increase my eye lubrication to prevent it drying out. *Another thing to add to my rehab regime. Great.* He warns me it's either that or resorting to Dad cling-wrapping it each night or, much worse, it being super-glued shut. At least in the quick consultation I've also learnt that my right eye's ability to track has improved. *Dad's wait has been worth it.*

Dad dropped me home and Gavin, my private physiotherapist, arrived. I'd decided that these weekly physio sessions were the only way I could speed up my recovery. I wanted to be challenged now and knew that I had to be the driver of my own rehab for it to be effective. So I organised my own team. As well as the new dynamic physio, there was my sister-in-law, Rach, and my childhood friend, Em. They were all great motivators and with them I felt safe to challenge myself. Also, they would come to me, which meant I didn't have to battle with transport or sit in waiting rooms.

We established a goal. I would walk without my frame down the aisle at my twin sister's wedding. I was to be her Maid of Honour in April 2008. Although this would be incredibly taxing, it would mean I would look less disabled, so it was a price I was willing to pay. Now I had nine months to make it all happen. Same length as a pregnancy, I couldn't help thinking.

~

Today my physio convinces me to go beyond the safety of my unit. I walk 100 metres up the street with one crutch, tackling uneven surfaces, wind and leaves for 20 long minutes. On the way back he asks me not to speak, and the walk only takes half as long. We spend the remainder of the session crossing the road back and forth and stepping up and down the curb, over and over again until my brain is so foggy with fatigue my body can't physically perform any longer. He senses my frustration and tiredness and says, "Good work, Em. Let's go inside and chat about where to go from here."

Returning to the quietness and safety of my unit, I sit in my chair to support my wobbly, tired head.

"What terrifies you most, Em?" he asks, reaching into his backpack, grabbing a pen and note pad.

At Talbot I would've been unable and unwilling to answer this question honestly. "Everything … I hope that note pad is big," I laugh.

But he just looks at me seriously and poises his pen ready to catch my list. I close my eyes and recall all that I now avoid. "Trams, crossing roads, changing direction, talking when I walk, stairs, carrying things, going downhill … Oh and then there's what I find hard … um assuming a split stance, sitting or standing, moving my arms and not causing my head to wobble."

He keeps writing and nods.

"That enough?" I ask.

"Yep, gotta go, Kiddo," he says, zipping his backpack up and throwing it over his shoulder. "Focus on the long term; let me worry about the short term," he says, locking the door behind him, leaving me feeling my rehab future is in safe hands.

~

For the next nine months my days were full, practising stairs, walking back and forth on the flat spongy cricket pitch on the oval opposite my place, swimming laps or doing Pilates. Also in my spare time as a lady of leisure I joined my local gym and began a weights regime along with a few aerobics and spinning classes. I'd stand at the front near the mirror and rail, trying hard to keep up with the rest of the participants. The different sequences were trapped inside my head and interpreted by my body in a delayed, uncoordinated, wobbly way.

A few months into this regime I began to experience the yo-yo nature of rehabilitation – from stroke survivor to stroke victim back to stroke survivor. It was overwhelming to realise the possibilities I'd opened up by forcing myself out of my comfort zone. I could now walk a short distance unaided on a flat surface in a rigid robotic way. But while walking like this I couldn't give eye contact, move fast or carry anything. Mentally drained, half of me squirmed at the future work I'd created. But the other half was so excited.

At Bec's wedding I almost achieved my goal of walking down the aisle without my frame. I needed to link arms with another bridesmaid. It was a fantastic day, but my elation was short-lived. After all those months of monotonous daily exercises, not quite reaching this milestone left me unsatisfied. *I probably looked more wobbly than usual in my attempt to not fall flat on my face!* Despite everyone's praise, I felt alone with my unfulfilled dreams.

The big day was over. My twin sister departed on her honeymoon adventure and I felt left behind. I'd worked so hard towards that day and I now felt as if I had no direction, no purpose. I kept going with my rigorous routine, but without a specific goal the effort didn't seem worthwhile.

I was slowly beginning to see the domino effect that the intense rehab was having on my other deficits. While I could walk with a stick now, it triggered my left arm nerve pain, led to sleepless nights and heightened my fatigue, fear and frustration. As a very active person in my former life, I hated that I couldn't perform at the same level.

My motivation gradually flagged and soon my regime began to fall apart. It was taking too much of a toll on my life. *Everyone around me expected me to keep improving, that I'd now throw away my walking frame and graduate to a stick.* I tried hard to fit in with those expectations, forcing myself to only use the frame when I was inside or alone, but the pressure I was putting on myself was too great. I was beginning to avoid my team because I didn't want to disappoint them or remind myself of what I'd failed to achieve. Had it become 'their' goal rather than mine, I wondered. I began to question whether I was setting myself up for failure by being so focused on walking unaided.

CHAPTER 31
Searching for Purpose

Two and a half years after my stroke, although I had made a lot of physical progress, the prospect of spending every day of my life just doing exercises began to terrify me. I was tired of my life being about rehab and needed to find a new direction and contribute to the world again. I was still young, had a degree and was highly motivated.

I had begun a journalism course by correspondence and was doing voluntary work for Scope Victoria's online communities. Scope, a not-for-profit organisation that provides disability services in Victoria, was formerly known as the Spastic Society. As I couldn't easily physically contribute to my new world, I relearnt how to operate a computer and type, and started using the online world to communicate. This was a huge leap in connecting me to others and helping me participate in life again. My own experience of face-to-face support groups had been physically and emotionally taxing, and I knew there was little support available for young survivors. Now I wanted to ensure that others feeling isolated would feel supported as well.

With the help of Bec, who was still overseas, I started Shoestrings, a charity organisation designed to support the thousands of individuals who feel isolated as a result of a particular experience. Shoes and shoestrings are things we all have in common, so these created the concept of Shoestrings, its motto being "Sharing souls and tying communities together".

The inaugural Shoestrings event was a photography exhibition held over a fortnight in an arts centre in Richmond. It involved communities impacted by stroke, whether it be a cleaner, neighbour, doctor, family member or survivors themselves, submitting a photograph of themselves with a pair of their shoes and writing a short summary about their experience and what they'd learnt. This was mine:

My Bachelor of Occupational Therapy, trip to Africa and long-distance runs did not equip me for stroking at 24 years of age. Nothing prepared me for life as a patient. However, now as a stroke survivor, I've found sharing has become the armour in my battle. 'Shoestrings' as an organisation stems from all I've learnt from the power of sharing. I hope that Shoestrings enables others to feel less alone. With 'shoestrings tight', I believe through sharing we can run this obstacle course together.

One hundred images were then enlarged and printed in black and white, with only the shoes in colour. They were then mounted and displayed on the walls of the exhibition space. Each of these photographs was sold and, together with ticket sales and a silent auction, we raised stroke awareness and funds for the National Stroke Foundation.

In the months leading up to the first Shoestrings event I was busy delegating tasks among all my networks to make the exhibition happen, with Bec helping from overseas. She broke down the tasks into realistic chunks, organised a Shoestrings team and sent through agendas and spread sheets to help us. She even liaised with the National Stroke Foundation on my behalf.

Seeing the incredible effort she had invested made me determined to do all I could to make it worth her while. I went along to small group meetings to encourage those impacted by stroke to submit their photographs and attend the event, and networked widely to get donations for a silent auction and generate ticket sales for the opening night. Promoting the exhibition was extremely daunting and tiring but fantastic for getting me out of my comfort zone and into the world again.

I wrote in my blog:

I spoke about Shoestrings to a 'Coffee Bean' group today. I must admit, the fact that 'coffee' was in the group's title made agreeing to speak a lot easier. I secretly hoped that they were all caffeine addicts and their morning Lavazza fix would keep them wide awake when listening to my monotonous soft voice. Ever since my stroke I've been quite keen to begin public speaking. My mum even borrowed a library book, Public Speaking for Wimps. However, sitting to read my talk in my Coke-bottle glasses with a soft, monotonous, unclear voice and maintaining little eye contact was a huge 'no no' in the public-speaking world. Thankfully, I detected no nudges, snoring or sudden head drops. If I ever get into the public-speaking domain, remind me to get coffee companies to sponsor me!

Incredibly, as a surprise, Bec flew from London for the Shoestrings opening night. I was literally speechless, but had committed to giving a brief three-minute thank you to the 100+ people who attended. Although I couldn't speak very well, the response I received and the connection I felt with the audience was exhilarating. This was the elation I had missed since my stroke. At that moment I wished my ability to communicate was good enough to pursue my newfound love of public speaking.

The day after the event an article was published in a magazine:

"Every now and then we see, hear or experience something that really makes us stop and think. Often these experiences are chosen to be kept to ourselves, however when I attended a very heartfelt and inspiring charity event early this week, I was so moved and inspired that I see no better way of sharing this with you.

Shoestrings came from the experiences of Emma Gee, who is currently going through rehabilitation post-stroke after being diagnosed with a congenital AVM (arteriovenous malformation). (Shoestrings definition of AVM was that Em's brain was like a heap of shoelaces … one just had a knot in it! All the blood pumped into that instead of flowing through her normal laces and the pressure of all that blood going into the one knot meant that surgeons had to clamp it to avoid it bursting!)

It wasn't until Emma Gee spoke so passionately and positively about her experience that it really hit the spot. Not a dry eye in the room, but not for sympathy … for admiration. Overcoming challenges, seeing that the glass is half-full and embracing the fact that life is not ruined, just adjusted accordingly …"

The event was more successful than I could ever have imagined. It raised funds and awareness, it forced me to network with other professionals and it unmasked a personal passion to share the knowledge that lay dormant in my disabled body.

Even before this I had known that my days with rehab and volunteer work were not enough. People frequently said things like, "You've been through enough, Em, just enjoy not working." They meant well, but they didn't understand how trapped I felt. During that Shoestrings speech, I saw a glimpse of a future for myself. I realised the value of my story, and what I could now offer to others.

But I had a long way to go. I decided to challenge myself by doing some casual marking for the OT Department at La Trobe University. I was so appreciative of the opportunity and it meant I could work from home. I knew what to write but my illegible writing was a problem. It was embarrassing to imagine the students' dismayed and disapproving looks when they saw my childlike handwriting.

There was the occasional opportunity to speak to OT students in their 'living with a disability' module. Again, when telling my story to a group, I had a similar exhilarating feeling to that I'd experienced when I spoke at the Shoestrings event.

Dad drove me to all my speaking engagements. In the car afterwards he would sense my huge mood lift and often say, "Whatever you just did in there, keep doing it, Em."

Later, I received an email from one of the students that only fuelled my passion to keep speaking. She ended the email with this line, "I will be a better OT because of you."

I became determined to branch out further into the world. After all, I did actually have a job to return to. My position at the Royal Melbourne Hospital was still open for me, and they were even willing to modify my role to suit my new capabilities.

But after my La Trobe experience, and knowing what my old job involved, it was obvious to me I wouldn't be up to it physically. Emotionally, it also felt like a backward step. Although it had been a safety net knowing the job was there, if I returned I would really just be holding onto the dregs of my former role. Facing a blank canvas was scary, but those close to me encouraged me to resign and move on. They were reassuring. "Em, your insights as a therapist *and* a patient will be invaluable in a future role."

In spite of my disability I assumed that with my degree, knowledge and experience in this area as an OT, and my eagerness to return to work, this next step would be a cinch. But it turned out to be one of the biggest learning curves I had to face. I had heard awful things about the entire job-seeking process from my patients, but never truly understood the hoops I'd have to jump through.

First I had to get a doctor's certificate from my neurologist to prove that I had a chronic medical condition. This was needed to get a Job Capacity Assessment at Centrelink. That assessment left me deflated, gutted. Once again, they'd focused only on what I *couldn't* do.

Then came the job-seeking phase, months of waiting and being passed from one consultant to another before I secured my first return-to-work trial. *At last I was about to enter the workforce.* I'd brainstormed, anticipated and addressed all the likely obstacles. Sure, I had physical limitations but I'd bought a scooter to overcome my mobility issues and figured out how I could use my electronic organiser to avoid handwriting. I also planned to increase my hours gradually, so fatigue wouldn't be an issue. But then a week before I was due to start, my potential employer reneged. There I was, desperate to work and feeling totally powerless! It was a huge slap in the face. I remember being in tears on the phone to my consultant, "I'm so keen to work that I'd be happy to collect 20-cent pieces in a car park."

After that I gave up on Centrelink and decided to resume job seeking on my own. Voluntary work led to casual paid work at La Trobe University again, but this time on campus. The OT department staff were extremely supportive but I was inwardly frustrated that the tasks I was doing were slightly demeaning. Admin and marking were all I was suited to with my physical issues and poor communication skills. My voice was still very soft and my words indistinct. I struggled to maintain eye contact because of my vision (looking up made my world spin), and all of these things depleted my already low confidence.

I needed to take a plunge and try something different. So I enrolled in a public-speaking course at TAFE, thinking if I could fix my inability to clearly communicate, I'd be able to return to OT work once again. But it was not that easy…

"So move your arms like this and pace back and forth and then stand still." The tutor walked as he spoke, demonstrating these actions. One by one the entire group took turns mirroring his different techniques. When it came to my turn, he just looked bewildered at my limp body and my walking frame and said, "Perhaps just watch, Emma."

After that course I realised that improving my communication skills was only likely to happen if I sought individual guidance. I met professional speaker Paddy Spruce, who helped me unleash my trapped story. With his face-to-face coaching, I began to adapt how I presented to my audiences. I bought a microphone to project my voice, sat when I spoke to compensate for my poor balance, bought a smart business wardrobe, and practised my speaking on anyone who would listen. I sought out familiar audiences, including my old workplace.

"You don't need to dress up for us, Em," my former colleagues would say. But dressing up in a suit and caring about what I looked like hugely improved my confidence. The muscles on the right side of my face were still paralysed, affecting my speech and appearance. Instead of undergoing invasive treatment like skin grafts, I decided to trial a Botox regime administered by Ian Carlisle, a remarkably generous and gifted plastic surgeon. Even though I felt like a human pincushion, Botox injections into the left side of my face seesawed my facial muscles and forced the paralysed ones to work. I also trialled a subcutaneous filler injected into my right cheek and moulded like wall putty across my now-atrophied facial muscles. Not only did I appear more normal, talking and eating were easier. An added bonus was that my pool goggles suctioned properly onto my now more symmetrical face, resulting in fewer eye infections.

I finally felt I was transforming myself, moving at last into a new and almost exciting phase of my life.

Chapter 32
Moulding a New Identity and Direction

Being a young woman, it was my appearance that worried me most at that time. In the first period after the stroke I wore stick-on prism glasses that made it seem I was viewing the world through venetian blinds. I looked like I was off to see a 3D movie. After tolerating this for a few months, I happily forked out my disability pension to pay for a pair of permanent glasses. These 'Coke-bottle plus' contraptions did the job of fusing my two worlds, but I was still self-conscious about the image they conveyed. I confess to taking them off and preferring to put up with my spinning double vision rather than copping strangers' stares. Besides, they were so thick that the weight of them hurt my nose.

The immediate benefits of undergoing Botox made me eager to explore other procedures. As soon as I could, I opted for squint surgery to realign my eyes and correct my double vision. This involved detaching and shortening the muscle on the right side of my eye to swing the eye to the right, and align it with my other eye. Despite fearing surgery in case I had another stroke, I was actually excited to have this procedure. In my head I would wake seeing only one world again, my visual deficits reversed.

I enter a booth, a combination of a department-store change-room and a toilet cubicle. The nurse instructs me to sit up on the sickbay-like vinyl bed beside a pile of brown-paper bags and white, folded gowns. She looks down at her clipboard. "Any history of diabetes, heart disease, back problems, arthritis … stroke?"

I satisfyingly answer loudly No to all but stroke. With each condition she purses her lips in disbelief, moving her poised pen from hovering over the 'Yes' box to the 'No' box. The questions eventually finish and my blood pressure is checked. I emerge from the booth in a now-familiar outfit – the see-through gown with a split up the back, the blue elastic shower cap and matching booties.

Exhausted from dressing, I collapse onto a grey plastic chair, joining the other vulnerable white-gowned people. This is the perfect environment to breed nervousness, all of us stripped of our uniqueness. I mentally re-dress them. The man to my left in a dark grey business suit, the lady ahead of me in bright pink with matching lipstick, the elderly man to my right, warm in a brown-checked sports jacket. I smile to myself.

Every other patient has an arrow marked on their forehead above their left or right eye. Everyone but me. I anxiously scan the room for an explanation. A sign on the wall to my right reads that all patients are marked to indicate to the surgeon which eye is to be operated on. *Why don't I have one? Is my right-sided paralysis identifying enough?* I am nervous, yet thankful it's my eye not my brain that's about to be operated on.

"Right eye?" my surgeon asks, while a nurse helps him tie his blue gown.

I answer immediately, "Definitely the right one!" I try to accurately point my ataxic finger to my right eye in case he can't tell his left from his right. I feel an urge to escape, a need for some familiarity. The nurse holds my tense and freezing left hand while the anaesthetist injects cold fluid into a vein in my right hand. A rush of anxiety suddenly engulfs my bloodstream and I'm forced to surrender.

I wake up an hour or so later in the recovery room. After wriggling my toes and circling both wrists, I fall back asleep – assured I have not had another stroke. But the procedure is not complete. Soon after, my surgeon returns to tweak the adjustable sutures to alleviate any double vision. My dad is standing at the end of my bed.

"What can you see?" my surgeon asks.

I see two Dads still … only now one is shadowed; the blurry image is on top of the other instead of beside it.

"Um Dad, actually two of him ... two stethoscopes ... two of you … so still double," I say quietly in disbelief.

"Overcorrection," my surgeon says, puzzled, glancing at his assistant while pulling the eye muscle a little and tugging the black stitch with tweezers.

"How about now?" he queries.

"Dad's now kind of single but he has two heads!"

The surgeon doesn't respond, just completes the procedure by tying a knot in the black thread. It's a done deal, my wonky vision now permanent. Dad crosses his arms and observes my nightmare from afar. My mum and brother enter. They look concerned and sad for me. No one says anything but everyone seems to know the surgery hasn't gone to plan. Mum's eyes well up empathetically, and I quickly catch the tear I feel escaping down my left cheek. *I have to be brave. Once I cry, I know I won't stop.*

After all my visitors have left, my tears erupt. I walk to the bathroom and glance again in the mirror. Yep, it's true. The surgery has aesthetically straightened my eyes. But it has also over-corrected my double vision, moving it from a horizontal to a vertical plane. Where I'd once viewed a person's cloned head on their shoulders, it now sat anatomically wrong on top of their heads! Suddenly, my brain has to readjust to a different view of the world. I may appear more normal, but am destined to continue to view the world in a distorted way.

~

The operation could have been attempted again when things settled, but as my eye was prone to ulceration, this was not encouraged. I had hoped the spinning would also be fixed. It wasn't. They suggested anti-seizure medication for this but I'd tried it before for my pain and knew it only worsened my balance.

In spite of these setbacks, my speech and endurance were improving and I was gaining lots of experience in front of audiences, doing free talks at places like Toastmasters, Rotary and Probus. I continued to network with other speaking organisations. My passion to share my story to a wider network only became stronger. With Paddy's help I learnt to present without a script so I could give my audiences eye contact, and I developed new topics, drawing on my experiences since the stroke. For example, with health providers I focused on client-centred practice, and with school students I would talk about resilience.

Soon enough I was networking with larger groups of people, at times very intimidating audiences. Although daunting, I approached each event as a personal challenge. *I need to advocate for all those people with disabilities. Try to break the disabled stereotype.* I loved this work but I could only do it occasionally, as retelling my story was emotionally and physically taxing.

At the same time I decided to begin a Masters Degree in OT at La Trobe University. It would enable me to one day teach OT students, and would give me the credibility to prove to people that there was an intelligent mind trapped inside my new disabled body. The decision boosted my confidence even more – I felt that I was beginning to shape a new identity for myself.

But life was very different this time around at La Trobe, the university where I'd taken my original degree. Now I had to be hyper-aware of things I had never noticed before, like where the stairs and disabled toilets were. Study itself had new challenges. Articles had to be converted to large font or audio for me. In spite of the constant support from the OT department staff and the disability advisor I was often given the material late or not at all.

The energy I exerted trying to access the material I needed heightened my frustration. I felt overwhelmed and isolated. The toll of studying began to compromise the balance in my life. Study deadlines meant I was pushing aside what I valued most, family and friends. The balance had shifted and now I was not getting enough time for rehab. After two semesters I made the difficult decision to defer. After being so keen to prove to others that it was possible to study again, it felt as though I was giving up. But I told myself, "I can make more of a difference now, drawing on my experiences as a therapist and a patient, than I can by studying for years for yet another degree."

Chapter 33
A New Love Life

At the same time I was experiencing these setbacks at university, I was doing some voluntary work at the National Stroke Foundation, and I unexpectedly landed into my first post-stroke relationship. He was also a stroke survivor. Our relationship began with a phone call. I was self-conscious about my slurred speech, but the ease of the conversation and the huge amount we had in common counteracted the nerves I felt when speaking on the phone. He was interstate and we got on so well that he suggested a Melbourne visit and reassured me that how I looked didn't matter. I knew he had very few physical side effects from his stroke, and I repeatedly warned him of all my visible disabilities, dreading that once he saw me face to face he would quickly leave.

He flew to Melbourne and, to my surprise, seemed romantically interested and a relationship developed. The fact that a good-looking guy found me attractive in my new disabled shell was both flattering and terrifying.

In theory it was great to have a boyfriend again, and I became swept up in the idea of someone actually liking me. But in practice it was a completely different experience to the relationships I'd had before my stroke. It was difficult meeting his family and friends, trying not to be a high-maintenance girlfriend. When I stayed with him interstate I'd leave my frame at his home when we went out, and he'd hold me up and guide my steps. It made me feel like a rag doll, but less like a disabled girlfriend. As the relationship progressed I became emotionally and physically reliant on him. I continually needed to hear his reassurance that image didn't matter. To his huge credit, he took the broken Em and tried to fix her. He challenged me to be myself and not hide behind the disability label. He urged me to see that my physical limitations weren't an excuse not to achieve, but a reason to achieve.

At the time, though, I was still in my own disabled bubble, refusing to move on. One of his friends once said to me, "Do you always introduce yourself and then go on to explain who you were prior to your stroke and why you are like you are now?"

My response was honest, saying that I'd rather people know straight away what's happened to prevent less speculation. But looking back now I see that the person I viewed myself to be no longer existed. I was trying to cling onto my old identity. I needed to move forward.

It was refreshing to return to dating and I floated along, dismissing my gut instincts that the relationship wasn't right. The reality was that we were not compatible. I believed that I had to tolerate his shortcomings because he had to put up with so many of my own flaws. When he complimented me I doubted his sincerity because my self-esteem was so damaged. I wasn't able to see how anyone would like me when I had become *this.* I admired his trying to prove me wrong, but ultimately when I had such a huge amount of self-doubt, there was no way I could reciprocate. Eventually we split, and in spite of how distressing that break was at the time, on looking back I can see it taught me a lot. Those around me couldn't commit until I could see past my disability and begin to see my own worth. It was comforting to know that whether or not I'd ever enter a relationship again, at least it was possible.

In a way breaking up was a relief. After factoring another person into my lifestyle, it felt good to focus once again on my own needs. Though devastated that the relationship didn't continue, it made me determined to build on my own strengths and create a different pathway. It also made me realise the importance of reciprocating in my other relationships.

Those around me were trying hard to pick me back up and include me in their lives. My two close friends actually asked me to give speeches at their weddings. I decided to snap out of my negative mindset. I started going to hairdressers to have my hair done. I began joining my friends on the dance floor. Although I was reliant on holding their thumbs to balance while I tried to bop to the tune, the inclusive feeling was invigorating. I was often the last one standing and I think often responsible for getting many extra people up on the dance floor. "If she can get up there and dance that badly, I can for sure!"

Chapter 34
A Real Working Girl Again

The media and fundraising I had done for Shoestrings strengthened my connections with the National Stroke Foundation and in March 2009 I started working part-time there as an Online Project Officer in stroke support. This involved developing a national online program in the form of an interactive discussion forum for the stroke community. It was a place where people who had been affected by stroke, from carers to therapists to siblings and stroke survivors, could share their stories and know that they were not alone. Because my role was largely computer-based, my inability to write wasn't a problem and I was able to mingle with both consumers and colleagues again.

At the same time I could run my own speaking business, still presenting approximately every fortnight, and able to work from home when I needed to. The flexibility of my role was perfect, especially considering all my medical appointments and my rehab schedule. The only drawback was the inevitable problem of accessing non-accessible bathrooms. But … *I was a working girl again.*

"There you go, Em, have a good day," the waiter at the café near my workplace would say, positioning my take-away coffee cup with a straw into my frame's cup holder. After a few months of adapting to my new work routine, I was finally able to enjoy my morning coffee at my desk again. As a coffee drinker now unable to carry a cup, this clever addition to my frame was amazing. My caffeine hit became my incentive to clamber up the steep hill of Queen Street. I even learnt that my frame's wheels fitted nicely in the cracks of the bitumen path's surface, making it easier to glide along so the hike was faster and safer. While getting into the city was a huge feat at first, my new employer was very accommodating, letting me come into the office later to avoid the city's peak hour.

"Morning!" I would say to my colleague already at her desk. "Embarrassing, but do you think I could get you to zip up the last bit of my suit?" I would hunch my shoulders to take off my black winter jacket, revealing the gap. "Sure, Em", she'd say.

Feeling tired from my early start, I would stagger down the corridor, flick on the fluoro lights and sit down in my high-back, supportive desk chair. I'd turn on my extra large desktop monitor and enter my new password, *Ilovemyjob*. Choosing a positive password forced me to start the day in an optimistic light. The inappropriate comments by commuters, the tiredness I felt from a night battling my pain or slipping on the route to work, were soon forgotten. In this bright frame of mind, I began my day.

However, my positivity was tested by the sight of my metallic-blue crutch leaning on my office desk. It was a constant reminder of the rehab I should be doing. I had the best intentions of incorporating it into my work day, but walking with a stick when you're carrying folders, trying to get to a meeting on time, or to get to the toilet quickly, was not realistic. Concentrating on my gait was *not* a priority. I began to resort to using my faithful frame in the office, but I felt guilty doing so.

Ever since Bec's wedding I had found it hard to shake off the expectation that I should be graduating to a stick. Trying to balance work, rehab and play was impossible. *What a bad role model I was for other stroke survivors*. I wanted to leave my disabled body behind and focus on helping others impacted by stroke. But I couldn't.

Approximately three years after my stroke my pain peaked and started to significantly hinder my life. I investigated a new procedure called deep brain stimulation. It involved further brain surgery to rewire the nerves. The surgeon was confident in carrying out the procedure, but there was no evidence that it would reduce my pain as, to date, it had only been used on patients with Parkinson's disease. This seemed too much of a risk. I felt stuck and helpless. Although I had a job, the cost of seeking opinions was immense and wasn't getting rid of my disability.

Thank goodness at the time I was in the care of an amazing private physiotherapist, Janet. Not only did she help me manage my pain physically, I could vent about the emotional burdens of my new life. I was beginning to see how they would also travel with me and needed to be addressed. Yet in the busy-ness of life, there was little space to complain to my close network. I wanted the time I spent with friends and family to be enjoyable.

Eventually I found a great psychologist, Julie. Meeting with her gave me a scheduled, uninterrupted space where I could selfishly let off steam about the many frustrations in my life.

Scheduling this time also ensured that I didn't bottle things up and that I didn't unnecessarily burden those close to me.

I also began treatments with Jared, an osteopath, and looked into mindfulness strategies like meditation and yoga, choosing to self-manage my rehab. I needed to be aware of my own needs if I was to perform at my best. Eye infections, medical appointments, pain management, waves of fatigue, sleepless nights and the emotional toll had to be factored in. I had to control them rather than let *them* control me. These new strategies provided a level of awareness and led to clarity and a sense of calmness and control over my life.

Going away alone was another technique for rebalancing my life. Although I loved time away with my close family and friends, I realised I was exerting so much energy worrying that I was spoiling their holiday that the stress outweighed the pleasure. I began taking lone trips to Gwinganna Lifestyle Retreat, a well-known resort in the hinterland of south-eastern Queensland.

Another way to refuel was by staying at my auntie and uncle's home in Sydney. My auntie is an important role model in my life. She has an endearingly positive outlook, considering the many personal health obstacles she's had to tackle. My uncle is a constant driver in my life, too, challenging me with goals that many automatically dismiss. Returning to my own routine after these visits, I felt more equipped to face ongoing obstacles. Being a working girl again and helping others was only going to be possible if I took good care of my own needs.

Chapter 35
Independence Tested

In 2011, six years after my stroke, my parents (and main caregivers) decided to move to the country to enjoy the delayed 'child-free' retirement that they definitely deserved. Dad's renewed enthusiasm for life in the country reminded me what I'd taken from them when he retired to be my full-time carer.

When they sold the family home, 10 minutes away from my unit, they also took a big chunk of my support with them. I realised how many little things they'd done for me. With my parents leaving, I had to delegate my support. I hated burdening others, particularly my siblings. For several months after my parents left, I tried to live pretending I didn't need anyone to help me. I stubbornly refused to accept or even ask for help, and didn't want to become reliant on strangers and feel the need to repay them for their support. Jobs like putting out the rubbish and cleaning up dog poo I had gradually let my parents do without feeling too guilty. Now when friends came around to see me I had to ask them to do these tasks, eating into our catch-up time. It seemed to unbalance the relationship, them becoming more like carers in my eyes. Also, I'd be taking that caring role away from my parents, and I wanted them to have a reason to come back to me.

This mindset made everything feel too hard and I progressively became more resentful towards my parents. They would return, and in the small window of time we had together, I'd unconsciously (and consciously) remind them of all the extra obstacles I now had since their move. This negative thinking fed my resentment. They'd leave and I'd be left with the guilt.

After accidentally locking my keys inside my unit three times in a row and flooding my laundry twice, I realised I couldn't rely on my parents' frequent but irregular visits to help me. I had to structure formal supports into my life. I told myself to snap out of it and began to notice the positives. *Gratefulness and resentment can't co-exist*. Gradually, I became grateful for my parents' input rather than critical of their oversights.

I gave spare keys to friends, had a friend mind my dog Gilbert when I travelled, began shopping online, caught more cabs and increased my weekly council homecare hours. My siblings and close friends happily took on many of the tasks that my parents had previously done. All these changes empowered me to live independently and I'm sure my parents didn't feel as guilty. I saw that by asking for and accepting support, I could achieve a lot more in my day. I became reliant on my parents more for emotional support, through reassuring phone calls or chats over Melbourne coffees when they came to town.

At times I'd retreat to their place in the country to rest and refuel. Here, I was happy to give up my fierce independence and lap up any TLC they could give. Their frequent, "Can I get you a cup of tea, Em?" and "What would you like me to cook for dinner, Em?" or "Can I do your washing?" helped revitalise my tired body and I'd happily let them take over. But in this relaxed state, I found that my brain completely shut down and my function was compromised. After each visit they'd drop my bags, Gilbert and me back at my unit then leave, and a tidal wave of sadness would hit. I would sit in eerie silence, feeling overwhelmed and desolate. I could tolerate these feelings, though, after the emotional recharge they'd given me.

As the years passed working at the National Stroke Foundation, I gradually adjusted to my parents' absence and seemed to restore balance in my personal and working life. Despite feeling finally able to contribute to society again, the longevity of my stroke began to kick in. My ongoing eye problems meant I eventually had to accept the involvement of Vision Australia, who helped modify my workplace.

Deb, my dedicated ophthalmologist, had suggested procedures to preserve my vision and slow the deterioration in my right eye. I'd opted to have a gold weight inserted into my right eyelid that had stubbornly refused to close since my stroke. This made my eyelid heavier and also added worth to the value of my body! Although invasive, this procedure reduced the number of eye infections, made blinking easier and allowing the lid closure needed to protect and moisten the right eye, preventing it from drying up further and dying.

My eye problems and lack of mobility remained a frustration, but my colleagues made my situation easier. "Afternoon, Em. Do you need me to put in eye drops?" or "Em, do you need anything from the café downstairs?" or "Want me to carry your things?" or "It's about to pour outside, Em. I'd leave now and work from home if I were you."

Although they were mindful of the practical difficulties I faced in my role, like enlarging tiny font size on a document, the invisible aspects were harder to recognise, and were often unintentionally overlooked. *How do you describe the impact of invisible symptoms such as chronic pain and ongoing fatigue?* I felt that burdening them with my physical needs was enough. Bringing attention to additional invisible problems would only highlight what I couldn't do.

I didn't want my disability to dictate my role. On one hand I craved their understanding and consideration. On the other hand I felt frustrated when they didn't treat me like a normal employee. Subconsciously I was becoming resentful. At times I chose to see their flexibility as being too accommodating. I wanted to be pushed, challenged and part of me questioned their intentions. I didn't want people to tiptoe around me. *This was my chance to make my stroke worthwhile, make a difference.*

Since returning to work, I had taken up any opportunity in the media to share my story. Through my involvement at La Trobe University and the OT department I was heavily involved in other projects and studies. I participated in research projects with my physiotherapist and plastic surgeon. Doing something now that might help others in the future made what I'd been through seem worthwhile.

My job at the National Stroke Foundation also gave me many opportunities to 'get out there'. They sought my input for many fundraising opportunities and campaigns. I had the privilege of meeting the Governor-General, The Honourable Quentin Bryce, at the launch of the Depression and Stroke DVD, a collaborative project between the foundation and Beyond Blue. In 2012 and 2014 I went to Parliament House, Canberra, with the Stroke Foundation to meet Members of Parliament in the 'Fight Stroke' campaign to increase awareness and funds from the Australian Government.

After four years I decided to take a career break from the foundation, as my vision was progressively deteriorating and I was struggling with the computer work. A large portion of my workload was sitting behind my desk and revolved around future programs. While this was suitable earlier on, I had outgrown my role as my abilities emerged over time. I now had more clarity about my purpose. My passion was to educate and advocate in a face-to-face capacity. My own speaking business had grown and my experience returning to work had reinforced my need to work directly with people.

Chapter 36
Out There and Advocating

The forced break from work gave me the headspace to reflect on what I was doing and why. I was able to invest my energy, time and vision into areas that were meaningful to me. It was an amazing opportunity to write, carry out voluntary work and focus on developing my speaking business through my website at www.emma-gee.com. After thousands of presentations, I no longer needed to read from a set script and loved the creativity of designing my own keynote presentations and tailoring the content to each audience. With practice, lots of experience and reflecting on my own journey, I was more flexible and able to quickly improvise if necessary.

Over the years I have been given the opportunity to work with varying groups from school and university students to health professionals to service providers and fellow patients. In all my presentations, I focus on both resilience and client-centred practice. I have also begun co-presenting workshops with other experts and health professionals. With their assistance and input I can be so much more effective in my delivery. It also enables me to travel more and work with larger groups as the effort required is shared. There's no way this would be possible if I did it solo.

The fact that my marketing is 90 per cent word of mouth means that I don't need to spend a lot of time on it. The business has grown to include a virtual administration assistant, a videographer and a bookkeeper. Paddy has become a strong mentor and is now my business manager. I seek his expertise particularly in developing new content and improving my negotiation skills.

With this kind of work, travelling has become a much bigger part of my life. Travelling with a disability is tough but essential to ensure I can reach as wide a network as possible. The trials and tribulations of travelling have now become part and parcel of my every day, and through my personal experiences I'm better able to advocate for others.

When I fly, I try to pre-empt the likely obstacles I may face, and almost over-plan. I know my walking frame weighs 7.6 kilograms for the check-in staff. I know that I beep when I walk through the security point, and I have figured out how to gorilla walk between the head rests down the aircraft aisle. But still each trip is a huge challenge and a steep learning curve. More often than not, an airport run goes like this…

After helping me zip up my bulging case and driving me to the airport, my wonderful regular cab driver double-parks at the drop-off zone and places my luggage inside the terminal door. From that point no one offers to carry my bags. I don't want to miss my flight, so I try to move my luggage myself. I hook my suitcase's pulley device over my frame's left handle grip and drape my black suit-bag over the other, cape-like. I yank it along sideways – crab-like. *A disobedient dog on a lead, refusing to co-operate!* After two shuffles forward, the weight of my suitcase tips my frame and all of us go over backwards. I land *splat* on top of my case, sandwiched between my suit-bag and my frame. Everyone stares. Vulnerable. On display. Helpless.

I realise people are too focused on their own plans or simply ignoring my plight. I need to get up. After heaving a shaky sigh, I tilt my torso backwards and throw my body towards my frame, squeezing the brakes tightly with both hands and heaving my body upright.

After previous trips I'm not surprised when the lady at the check-in says, "You have to pay for excess luggage if you want to take that on the aircraft, M'am." She points her chin at my frame. All airline policies specify that walking aids are excluded from the baggage weight, so rather than disagree with a staff member just doing their job, and miss my flight, I pay the charge. I often feel too tired to fight yet another small battle, but I'm aware that I need to advocate for others who don't have a voice. I make a mental note to write yet another letter to the airline to protest against this charge.

The next step, before a strong coffee, is passing the security metal detector. I line up and put my possessions in the blue trays provided. But I'm not fast enough and the queue banks up behind me. *I'm a stuck five-cent piece in a parking metre.*

"Walk on through, M'am," an airline staff member instructs loudly.

I don't move.

"Um … you need this to walk, right?" He taps my frame's handle-bars and then rocks it back and forth, teasing my independence.

Immediately I tighten my grip defensively and quickly reply, "Yes." *It's not a fashion statement.*

"How about I walk you through instead." He glides my frame through with a long beep then returns, rolls up his sleeves and holds out his hairy forearms. With my frame out of sight, I feel compelled to cling on and we waltz through. Standing, star-shaped, I'm padded down by a female stranger. *She's checking for dangerous goods that I may be disguising with my disability.* I collect my bags and make my way to the lift down to the gates.

Alone inside the lift I begin to notice the aches in my left hip from my fall. Suddenly, with a thud, the metal box I'm travelling in jerks to a stop. I wait … But after a few minutes I realise it's not going anywhere and neither am I. *I'm stuck in a lift!*

I press the 'emergency' button.

"Hi, it's Jessica. How are you today?" a cheery voice answers.

Then before I can respond, she says, "Do you mind holding?" and again before I can say a word 'call-waiting' music comes on. *Yep, in a lift. Yes, I've pressed an emergency button.* Then she doesn't come back. I press the button again and get the same spiel from a lady named Linda.

"What lift are you in, Dear?" she asks.

I bend down low to reach the speaker and talk loudly and slowly in the same demeaning way many strangers speak to me. "Melbourne Airport."

"So Melbourne University?" she asks. I can hear her typing.

"No, Melbourne Airport," I repeat even slower and louder.

Minutes pass … Male voices call instructions from above me and Linda's high-pitched voice squeaks other commands. The voices clash and morph into a cloud of confusion. *I don't understand anything anyone's saying.*

Then the crackling speaker fades and there's silence.

"Is anyone there?" I shout, but I can't project and no one answers. I start to panic. *No water and it's stuffy in here*. I take my jacket off and remind myself of my business motto, "*It's not what happens to you, it's how you choose to deal with it.*"

A perfect opportunity to practise what you preach, Em.

Suddenly the metal doors of the lift part.

"Are the doors opening?" a man above shouts.

They are. But, just like in the movies, all I see is a concrete wall and some cables.

"They're open but there's a wall," I try to shout back.

"Are you OK?" another lady joins in from the speaker. Once again I'm not sure who's asking what.

"Are you still in the lift?" a man shouts.

I'm confused. *How does he think I could escape?*

"Yes," I say, probably too forcefully.

Once again, silence. I hear a knocking sound and then nothing. Then a few male voices. Fifteen minutes later, which feels like three hours, the doors are forced open. All I see are three men's work boots in the opening, level with my head. One male voice instructs me, "Climb on up."

I just gaze down to my walking frame and after a short silence I see a guy's head peering down at me. Bewildered at who he is about to rescue he slowly says, "Umm … I'll come down and help you." He levers me up and his two colleagues drag me onto the shiny white surface of the airport floor.

Space. Air. Noise. "Thank you," I gasp.

After recovering from that adventure I board early with the 'people with special needs' announcement and hike to my designated seat, which is at the far end of the aircraft. Despite clearly stating I get tired and can't walk too far, they seem to assume I'll need my stint of rehab. The flight attendant then puts on my seatbelt for me and takes me step by step through the safety instructions.

After I hear this all again with my fellow passengers, we take off. Sitting for a prolonged length of time causes my nerve pain to peak and I always feel the need to move. On longer flights I've even resorted to walking up and down the aisle or lying on my back and putting my legs up the aircraft's walls.

Later in the flight, the attendant crouches down next to me in the aisle and says, "We'll be exiting this aircraft via the tarmac, would you like the special lift down?"

I have travelled once in that dodgy, terrifying cherry-picker-like lift machine and immediately reply, "No thanks, I can do stairs."

She nods.

We land. Once the seat-belt sign is off, my fellow passengers are on their digital devices and with the *click* of their belts, are released to resume life again.

I sit and watch them, my belt still fastened. I know from flights past that I'll depart with the staff and meet the cleaners on their way in.

"Sorry about the long wait, M'am. We had to wait for the special lift," the same attendant says.

"But I didn't ask for the lift. I can do stairs. I'd prefer stairs."

But the lift has been organised, as has a wheelchair. So I swallow my fear and frustration, plonk into the chair and take the dreaded lift.

Another airline staff member with giant earmuffs pushes the wheelchair across the tarmac. "Is someone meeting you?" he asks behind me.

"No, I'm travelling for work so I asked for assistance to the baggage claim and then onto the cab rank," I say.

Suddenly my wheelchair stops. "So no one's meeting you?" he asks, clearly annoyed.

"Well I'm boarding the next flight, we're very understaffed today and there's no people mover so you'll have to wait 30 minutes or so," he says in a hassled tone.

"Are you serious?" I ask.

No answer. He is gone.

I am left stranded in a dodgy non-self-propelling wheelchair facing a pole and a metal rubbish bin. I feel unheard, forgotten, demeaned and rejected. *A bit of rubbish that hadn't quite made the bin.* Others walk by, only stopping to dispose of their rubbish. Eventually a cleaner emptying the bin finds me. She volunteers to "do me a favour" (stressing that it's out of her hours and not in her job description) and escorts me to the baggage carousel. Vulnerable and desperate, I just nod and thank her.

Dumped at the carousel, I watch my suitcase, pink and lonely, revolving around and around on the black licorice-like conveyor belt. A stranger offers to lift it off for me. I thank my Good Samaritan and muster the energy to exit the terminal to the cab rank.

Arriving at my hotel exhausted, I want to double-check at reception that my room is definitely accessible. I had called earlier to request a 'disabled room' just to be sure.

The receptionist says, "Well it's not a disabled room, but it's a semi-accessible one."

I look at her, confused. "Sorry, what's the difference between the two?"

"Oh, it's accessible but I think um … well um, it has less rails," she says, clearly not knowing.

So what disability would I need to have to warrant me being given a fully 'disabled room'? I actually suspect accessible rooms don't exist at this venue. More often than not, although claiming to meet regulations, disabled bathrooms are used as storerooms or are locked. Typically, the designated 'accessible' room is far from safe and has rails randomly installed to attempt to meet the standards.

The hotel staff member leads me to my room, wheeling my suitcase and opening the door for me. Although it's modern and smoke-free, when I enter I see a massive staircase.

"Stairs!" I say dumbfounded.

She stands there with a big smile on her face. "Yes, M'am, we've upgraded you!"

"I can't do stairs with a walking frame," I whimper.

"Ohhhh sorry, Ma'am, but we have no other rooms tonight," she says.

So I peer up the big staircase. "I will crawl up these stairs, but if there's a fire come and get me."

Sheepishly, she leaves.

I leave my frame at the base of the stairs and take a deep, shuddering breath. I then hitch up my grey suit skirt, tuck my PJs under my arm, hold my toilet bag in my teeth and crawl.

Six months and many emails later, I was reimbursed for both my excess-baggage payment and my night in the 'semi-accessible room'. Hopefully my persistent attempts have helped educate service providers, heightened social inclusion and shown others what is possible.

Chapter 37
The Longevity of Stroke

As a naive stroke survivor I thought that over time things would slowly become easier and get better. But I have learnt that stroke is a never-ending story, particularly where my vision is concerned. Over the years my ophthalmologist has suggested ways to preserve my sight and slow the deterioration in my right eye. Despite religiously following her instructions to lubricate, cling-wrap, use an eye patch, etc. my vision has slowly worsened. Since my stroke my right eye has been drying out and slowly dying.

The end point in the race to save my eye is a tarsorrhaphy, but I have done everything in my power to avoid this. It is an old-school procedure where they stitch your eyelid partially closed, thus permanently shutting the eye and protecting it from further infection. After years of measures to normalise my image, the prospect of sewing my eye shut feels like giving up. Despite the difficulty of going against many experts' recommendations, I have decided not to go through with this procedure. I need to look at the situation holistically. The procedure would impact more areas in my life than my vision. My confidence, my youth, my image, would also be further compromised. Not having the surgery was the right decision for me.

I take full responsibility for how my eyesight is today. Having this ownership prevents me from blaming or living in the past and I find that complaining about the symptoms (that could've been prevented or delayed if I'd opted to have the procedure) isn't fair on those around me, and a waste of energy. *It is what it is.* I have opted to continue lubricating my eye, moistening the environment I'm in and even resorting to wearing my dreaded eye patch again at home.

Regardless of all that, I'm now basically blind in that eye. Over the years I've adjusted to focusing on the spinning vision I have in my left eye. I've sought advice about bionic eyes, nerve grafts and other options. Ophthalmology research is moving so fast. I remain optimistic that one day it will catch up with me.

My eyes are one of many ongoing health issues. I now take preventative measures like having annual flu vaccinations and continue with Botox injections. Another unexpected problem secondary to my stroke is the need to wear a plastic mouth guard at night. After a childhood wearing expensive braces, my atrophied jaw muscles are causing my perfectly aligned teeth to shift.

The financial toll is immense. Instead of saving for holidays or my kids' school fees, I'm paying for medical aids and procedures. What's more, I am not able to work as I once did. It's physically and emotionally taxing, but I have to factor in room to incorporate my ongoing stroke recovery needs. I am fortunate and reassured to know that my parents are always there for financial support should I need them. The stress that this lifts from my life is huge. Especially when Centrelink constantly suspends my pension, assuming I'm no longer disabled. I am forever grateful for the financial security so many others don't have.

Equipment is essential and I admit I choose to get aids that are not just functional but also younger looking and funkier. They're more expensive but they make having to use an aid at my age more bearable. It's easier to accept if it's one that's well designed and fashionable. Yes, even in the disabled world there is a fashion hierarchy! Unfortunately frames need replacing, which means forking out $700 to $800 every couple of years. My first frame was snapped in half like a chicken bone by an overly helpful stranger handling it. Mum drove over the second one with her four-wheel drive. The third frame rusted and the fourth one was *stolen* from my carport.

The longevity of stroke continues to test and challenge me. At times I feel the after effects of stroke just keep punishing me. Even eight years later, I needed more head surgery. The metal screw from the plate used in my craniotomy had rubbed on the arm of my glasses and become infected, needing to be removed. I was unable to wear glasses for months while it healed. I thought another operation and the associated dependence would hugely set me back. But maintaining important things in my life makes each difficulty much easier to withstand. Being a bridesmaid for one of my best friends, despite my having 'a screw loose', was both an honour and a great distraction.

While I've endured many physical obstacles so far, the emotional toll is often overlooked. Depression is the Siamese twin of stroke. Your mood fluctuates like a seesaw: high when something finally clicks after years of practice, low when you feel like you've gone backwards or need to ask for help.

None of the obstacles I've faced could have been dealt with without the incredible support network I'm lucky enough to have. Despite my stroke drastically changing the dynamics of our family, the way they all have supported me throughout my journey has been unbelievable. Mum and Dad are my all. Despite the distance, they frequently visit and are constantly there for me. They are not only my best supporters but also my best friends. And my siblings – they've never complained to me about me stealing my parents' attention from them, even though I still lie awake at night feeling guilty about it.

Bec has been a constant motivator in my life and I know will always be there for me. As my identical twin and with her 'anything's possible' mindset, she has provided me with a baseline. She has always challenged me. If I'm too sensitive, she tells me so, always reminding me to move forward and not to take things too seriously. I sometimes become jealous of her living the life I had planned, getting married and having three beautiful kids. But her new little family make me feel included in their life. In a way, her having a baby was the closest thing to me having my own children. Even today, three babies later, when she says, "Em, she's got our eyes," I feel a shiver of excitement and burst into a smile.

Now that Bec has a young family I seem to be the one with all the freedom. "Do yoga for me, Em," she'll say with a sigh, removing the pink lid of the play-dough with her teeth, stirring the pot of soup she's cooking on the stove while balancing her youngest on her hip. I leave the chaos, feeling guilty at having ample 'me time', off to yoga and a peaceful hot coffee to follow.

My brother Pete is very different to Bec. Over the years I have really come to rely on his opinions. He's very sensible, full of wisdom, and he rarely makes a quick decision; he examines the pros and cons of every situation. My sister-in-law Rach is unbelievably supportive and nurturing, while also very practical and straightforward. Over a cup of tea I often discuss an issue that is bothering me in my life, and Pete and Rach always give me their direct, very rational viewpoint. They have the ability to step aside and assess a situation and not get emotionally bogged down. I'm sure without their foresight, wisdom and guidance I would have made some bad decisions.

Although my older sister Kate lives interstate and is busy with her work and family, she has been a constant listener and enables me to live in the present. As OTs we have a lot in common. Although due to work commitments nowadays my stays there are less frequent, I still always feel so welcome in their home, their spare room even entitled Em's Room. My niece pointed out that they couldn't buy a certain house as there were, "Too many stairs for Emma."

At times when I have become too engulfed in an issue my many supporters have helped me to highlight the positives and put things in perspective. I recall Bec's words when I was contemplating whether or not to stitch my eye closed and struggling to find any optimism in the situation. "Look at the positives, Em … you'll have the blokes in the street lining up, thinking that you're winking at them," she said. Her attitude is contagious and reminds me that a sense of humour is essential.

Chapter 38
Life Now

Pain screams around my left side and rams into my throbbing joints, but I don't give my sleep-deprived body a chance to entertain the thought of staying in bed. After quickly meditating to get my mind in a positive state I throw my covers off and let the cold air continue to wake me. I dress my body before it realises we're going for an early swim. It's raining, but I know that moving my body is the only way to manage my pain and refuel my daily motivation. It's now my sole medication.

The lifeguard sees me and disappears into the pool storeroom to retrieve my flippers, running belt and neck float. Keeping them here saves me lugging them to and from the pool in a cab. He fights the rain and carries them to the pool's edge. "Looks like you're the only one braving this weather. Enjoy your swim, Em," he says with a smile. I leave my frame locked on the pool's edge and, after dangling my numb toes in the water, force myself to jump in.

~

Running is now replaced by swimming. I've grown to love it, enjoying the freedom of leaving my frame on land. I swim in a full-length wetsuit all year round, in rain or sunshine, to compensate for my warped body thermostat. I chuckle at fellow swimmers' puzzled looks when I enter the water in a 'wetty' on a 30-degree day. With experience the obstacles I'd faced in relearning to swim have now sunk out of sight and mind. They still exist but I can now float above them.

Swimming is my pain medication, and my anti-depressant. After years attempting to completely cure and rid myself of my nerve pain, I have finally accepted its presence. Rather than let its undeviating existence control me, I've become an observer of it. By acknowledging it, I've learnt to make room for it and try to distance it from my daily life. After religiously jotting down daily pain patterns for months in a diary, I have become aware of what triggers and exacerbates my pain. If I have niggling pain or am feeling flat or sluggish, I enter the water and imagine the negativity leaving my body like osmosis. Likewise, if my pain worsens I visualise kicking it out. I emerge from the pool feeling refreshed, refuelled and ready to tackle my day.

~

Once home, I hang my wetsuit up to dry, whack some more eye gel into my right eye and crawl to gather my laptop to do some work at the local café. Although my swim has dulled my nerve pain, a combo of the weather and tiredness still means it niggles. *Give me a break, body!* I plead. At least I have kick-started my motivation. A coffee will hopefully help and getting out will be a good distraction. I open my heavy front door by wedging my left elbow in the gap then squeeze through the opening and simultaneously grip and guide my frame. I shuffle to my scooter, Harley, my car substitute. He's very familiar with the route to my local coffee shop. I know the bumps in the footpath to dodge to make the trip faster. Eager for coffee, I switch the vehicle onto high speed (still turtle-slow) and glide down the hill. *Feeling so free. Moving forward and fast.* After years of trying to adapt to my life, I am beginning to feel more in control of things.

I park on the nature strip. A waiter sees me approach and comes out to help me.

"Hi Em, how's things today?" He carries my heavy red laptop bag inside and holds the door open for me. He places my bag on the brown booth seat. I trail behind him and sit beside it.

"Same coffee as usual, Em?" he asks, pouring me water and slipping in a straw.

I open my laptop to begin planning my next presentation. Crazy, but I love working in a noisy, chaotic environment. Despite having a home office, getting out among the background hum of people is easy, undemanding company. It's a routine I have incorporated into my day.

Nowadays, I typically café hop, writing and taking regular breaks for yoga, swimming or seeing friends. I spend the remainder of my day preparing for upcoming presentations, developing new content, meeting clients or fellow patients, doing voluntary work and research.

My iPhone beeps, signalling that I have a text. 'Congrats on doing that walk, Em." I smile and force myself to soak up the praise. To sustain motivation and remember to keep challenging myself is tough, especially when often I don't see a huge change in my performance. Many of my achievements are hard to celebrate. They were once so easy and are seen as a cinch to many around me. When you're continually trying to keep up with others it's hard to allow yourself time to *stop* and evaluate your achievements. Quite often I respond to others' congratulations sarcastically, failing to acknowledge the milestone. Instead I just keep going, striving for the next thing on my bucket list.

I admit to feeling a bit hard done by when an accomplished task is not recognised. I know that I have to announce this achievement, even though it seems like I'm bragging. As time has passed, and people's priorities have become so different to mine, it's even harder to get their attention. My achievements can easily float by unacknowledged.

After a few hours of work, I return home and loop Gilbert's red lead over my frame's handle and take him to the park to meet my niece and nephew for sushi. I adore all my nieces and nephews and I am forever grateful for the huge role I have in all their lives. While it scares me that there's less 'Auntie Em' time as the families all expand and age, I try to be the best auntie I can be. I can relate to their cries of frustration as they learn to speak or walk for the first time. But their staggering, rigid first steps are only temporary. As they've developed and mastered these milestones, I've secretly thought they'd run away and leave me behind when they could. But they surprise me every day with their understanding.

"Let's play *What's the time Mr Wolf*," my niece says. She jumps up and down on the spot, releasing any extra excitement by shaking her hands. In a high-pitched, breathless manner she tells her brother and me the instructions. "So what you do is when I yell, 'Dinner time!' you both run away from me so …"

She abruptly stops. She stands still. Scratches her head, frowns seemingly confused, looking back and forth from my frame to me. *She's realised that I can't run. How do I explain this?* Then suddenly she widens her eyes and says, "Oh umm. Auntie Emma you try to run, OK? Just hold onto your bike [aka frame] and pretend?" I'm chuffed at her problem-solving ability to include me. In fact, my frame is a novelty and they take turns to sit on it. Even when we cross the road, they hold onto the frame's handle as if it were my hand.

Over time, along with the trust and support of my siblings I've adapted how I do things. Changing nappies on the ground, wheeling my non-walking nephew in a block trolley to move him safely, transferring hot Milos from the microwave to the island bench on my walking frame's seat or taking my nieces on special outings to the movies via cabs. I proudly attend their kinder concerts or swimming classes and am silently thrilled that I'm always invited. In my mind, I am the luckiest auntie in the world.

At the park I veer off the even path, taking a shortcut across the bumpy grass to the tanbark area. I unleash Gilbert, leave my frame near the monkey bars and join my niece on the black web-like rope course.

"Do you think I can climb to the top?" I ask her.

"You'll do it easily, Auntie Em!"

I smile and try to make clambering up look easy, determined to make her see that anything's possible if you just give it a go. Maybe things are done differently, but they still can be accomplished.

After lunch, with tanbark-covered legs and blistered hands, I return to my home office to do another stint of work before my yoga class. My ears still ring with my niece's pleas to, "Watch this, Auntie Em!"

~

The prospect of a child-free future terrifies me. The physical toll pregnancy would place on my body, along with feeling that it'd be unfair to inflict my disability on my child, haunts me. But even if I never have children, I know I will have fewer regrets having shared these little ones.

I smile inwardly. I do love my life. Many wonder how I could, assuming that my quality of life would have been crushed when I acquired my disability. In fact, my new self only makes me appreciate life more. Every day I try to turn obstacles into opportunities. *You can't have a rainbow without rain*, I repeatedly chant to myself.

At times sustaining this mindset isn't easy. As an inspirational speaker it is assumed my motivation is never-ending. But I am human and need to stop sometimes to recharge. I now know that stopping forces you to reflect, something that is vital but so hard to do. I still see my psychologist occasionally. I also schedule in other breaks to reflect and refuel, whether it's returning to my parents' place, visiting my sister's family or relatives in New South Wales, or travelling alone. Without such circuit breakers I can't sustain what I do and maintain a balanced quality of life.

When travelling with friends, I need to organise trips with smaller groups of people. As time has gone on they have become so mindful of my extra needs. Hiring cars, carrying my luggage, making my bed, booking accessible accommodation or cooking my meals are just some of the things my friends now do that make holidays so much easier. Accepting their help is better than becoming frustrated or interpreting their kind offers as devaluing. I'm probably now a better travel partner.

As time goes on, the prospect of travelling and holidaying overseas with others has become less daunting. So many adventures, opportunities and possibilities are ahead of me.

Yoga is another opportunity to reflect on, which I have incorporated into my everyday life. Through yoga I can absorb all that I've done and at the same time calm my mind, like stilling a shaken-up glass snow dome and letting the white snowflakes settle. Afterwards I feel grounded, anchored and balanced.

~

My aqua yoga mat is rolled out for me in my usual spot and a fellow yogi places a purple block beside it. Walking unaided to reach this spot is always a challenge, dodging the other coloured mats and zig-zagging around tranquil flattened bodies. Sitting in a cross-legged position I heave a sigh of relief at not having fallen on anyone. I lie back to join the other yogis in their relaxed states. The placement of my mat in a little nook gives me a sense of security, comfort. Throughout my practice I can adapt all the instructed postures by latching onto the wall next to me, giving me that extra support.

The *shoulds* of challenging myself by attempting certain poses have been at the forefront of my mind. Although I've accepted my disability, I fear that I have become resigned to reaching my limit and that *this is it*. I need to keep pushing my limits. So today when the yoga instructor demonstrates a new pose and warns us that it will challenge our balance, I force myself to have a go. I take a deep breath, squeeze my eyes shut and in the middle of Warrior 3 I let go of the supporting wall. Next minute I'm on my back, tangled up in embarrassment, my glasses crooked, and me staring at the ceiling. The other yogis are standing in split stance, their weight evenly distributed. Balanced, so still and focused, as I try to work out how to untangle myself.

"Are you OK?" my yoga instructor whispers, concerned.

"I'm fine. I could do this last week so I thought I'd try again," I whisper. But my words don't come out as quietly as I had hoped and a few yogis turn. I crookedly grin. Once I would've wished my bruised ego and I could disappear into the mat. But today I'm glad I tried. I admit to being frustrated that it didn't eventuate like I'd planned. But I know that I'll get there with time and practice. The others around me keep going. When I'm ready, I take another deep breath and join them.

Chapter 39
Finding Where I Fit

At the tram stop an elderly lady lowers herself ever so slowly onto the green, splintered bench beside me. Her spine is so curved she doesn't even need to lean forward as she rummages through the handkerchiefs, jars of lollies and papers stowed in the wire basket under the black vinyl seat of her walking frame. She mutters loudly to herself and then turns stiffly towards me, eyeing my walking frame. "Do you find that your joints get achy, Dear?" she asks. "It's worse in this cold wind though, isn't it, Lovey." I just listen. Many people assume that I share their issues now that I roam around in a disabled shell and use a walking aid. And it's probably true.

~

I have become used to being sometimes ignored by my generation and pitied by those older than me, or automatically spoken to as if I'm their best chum. Today, any reference to the many similarities I share with another is a relief. Without speaking, there's already a mutual respect and acknowledgement of what we endure.

When I first started meeting younger stroke survivors, associating with their issues (the same ones I had faced early on) was confronting. All I could see was a mirror of deficits, our similarities rudely staring back at me. I would chat away brightly, highlighting the many positives we both needed to hear, but would leave feeling gutted and disheartened at our likenesses.

Now I have formed some great friendships with young survivors. I love the opportunity to give back, and to make them feel less alone. That mentor figure is something that I lacked in my own recovery. The whole process of helping them has become therapeutic for me as well. The commonality with fellow survivors is priceless. I don't need to explain what fatigue is, what nerve pain feels like and the effort involved in doing any task or achieving a milestone is automatically acknowledged. The yo-yo nature of recovery is understood – those days where you wake feeling disability-free followed by days of feeling like you're 90+ and just want to cry.

Many survivors have been left physically unscathed but struggle with other impacts of stroke, like memory loss or personality changes. I used to be jealous of people like them and their ability to return to their old life easily. I've since learnt that their scars may be invisible but impact them just as badly. Because many appear to be physically able, they are not eligible for rehab and community services. Although I might moan about rehab, it does make the transition from one life to another much smoother.

Having a physical disability is also easier for those around me to understand. It's visual proof that I'm not normal and at times a valid excuse if I'm tired or unable to join in. In fact, fellow survivors without physical deficits have resorted to carrying walking sticks to flag to strangers that they need to be mindful. Long term, the many invisible effects of stroke such as fatigue, chronic pain and frustration are definitely shared by many survivors.

Initially I was too unwell to exert energy into being angry. I was so reliant on those around me to fight on my behalf. Their forgiving, optimistic and forward-thinking attitudes certainly affected my outlook as I began to take control of my life again. In saying that, there have definitely been times throughout my recovery, and still are, where I feel bitter and frustrated. Nowadays this only seems to fuel my motivation to advocate for others. For me, I've learnt that focusing on and being angry about what I've lost is a waste of time and energy, although it's important to acknowledge my feelings of anger. I have found ways to vent. Whether it's through a yoga session, writing, or a chat with friends, I can still move forward despite the presence of these feelings. I had a stroke – no compensation or angst will change that.

Many ask if I get upset and irritated with some people's unhelpful actions and attitudes. Initially I was very frustrated and alone when I wasn't offered assistance with stairs or was not given a seat on public transport. It reinforced why many give up trying to feel accepted and included in society. But a few years into my recovery I met a paraplegic who changed my perspective on this. He said, "See it as an opportunity to educate, Em." From that day on, I began to try to view each obstacle as an opportunity. Nowadays if people ignore me (as pretending that they can't see my need is probably easier than not knowing what to do or say), rather than put my energy into getting irritated, I choose to ask for help and explain to them how they can assist me. Usually they happily oblige.

"Could you please help me lift my frame onto the tram?" I ask a fellow commuter at my tram stop.

"Sure … Very happy to … I guess I wasn't sure whether or not I should offer. Some people get err um, well, a bit offended," someone might say.

Many able people say that they are worried that in offering help to those with disabilities they have been judged as patronising. Some disabled people believe they are perceived as incapable if they accept or ask for help. But I believe this exacerbates the division between the able bodied and the disabled, the latter becoming more isolated and less integrated into society.

My mission is to show others like me that being themselves is enough, to get them to say proudly *I am still a person, I am just a person with a disability,* to show them that despite our ailments we can still live and love life; to encourage them to step out of their comfort zones and identify with the able-bodied people around them. Rather than focusing on what differentiates them and being resentful, I want them to look for likenesses with able-bodied people. The grief of losing 'who we were' is an ongoing process, but immersing ourselves in it only isolates us more.

Back at the tram stop a lady drops her pink purse near my foot. I reach down and pick it up. After years of being supported and people still doing so much for me while feeling so trapped, the chance to help another is refreshing. An opportunity to reciprocate the support that has largely driven me and has been, and still is, crucial in my recovery today.

She smiles and thanks me. I smile back.

How to Stay in Touch with Emma

For any questions or obtaining further information about booking Emma for your upcoming event please contact her via her website at emma-gee.com

Acknowledgements

I can't list all of the people who have contributed to my recovery and my life. The toll my condition has placed on others' lives is huge. But not a day goes by that I'm not aware of the massive sacrifices that many of you have made. I would not be where I am today without your care, dedication and assistance. You have ensured my life has balance and meaning. Thank you.

Thank you to Mr. McMahon, Professor Morgan and Elizabeth Ritson for saving my life. I am deeply grateful for your incredible skills and expertise, and that of the many other health professionals who have been instrumental in my recovery.

Particular thanks go to my incredible family. To my mum for the endless hours you sat by my side, supporting me, grounding me and giving me hope. Although it was grueling for us both, you helped me read, relive and articulate this story. Also to my dad, for your incredible wisdom, encouragement and support.

With gratitude to my siblings and their families for constantly refueling my motivation. Your support and belief in me has shown that anything's possible. A special thanks to Kate and Doug for your encouragement and advice during the editing process!

Also thank you to Paddy Spruce, my speaking mentor and friend, who helped me find my voice, communicate my message and kept me grounded.

And of course I am so appreciative of those involved in the publishing of this book. To my editor, Annie Hastwell, for her unwavering patience and dedication in helping me sift through my endless folders of writing. Your efforts enabling me to relay my story were extraordinary. Also to my publicist Deb and all those who reviewed my writing, providing me with such powerful endorsements which will help me convey my message to a wider audience. With special thanks to Julie and the OpenBook Creative team for your incredible skills, guidance and constant consultation, always striving for the best outcomes.